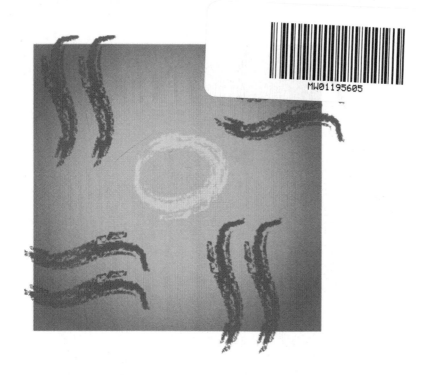

Wholistic Kinesiology

A QUICK AND EASY SYSTEM
FOR OPTIMIZING YOUR HEALTH

DR. J DUNN

ISBN: I-4I96-9828-I
ISBN-I3: 978I4I9698286

Visit www.booksurge.com to order additional copies.

WHOLISTIC KINESIOLOGY®
DR. J DUNN, FIRST EDITION

Wholistic Kinesiology®

"Miracles, in the sense of phenomena we cannot explain, surround us on every hand: life itself is the miracle of all miracles."

—

GEORGE BERNARD SHAW

TABLE OF CONTENTS

PART III: WHOLISTIC KINESIOLOGY: TECHNIQUES AND EXERCISES

FORWARD

I first heard of Dr. J Dunn while sitting on an airplane 30,000 feet in the air. Julie, the passenger next to me was telling me about her health crisis journey. We were lamenting the lack of good quality health care at the time, in the late 1990s, in New Mexico where we both lived. At the time I was looking for a top-notch doctor to add to what I like to call my personal "board of directors." These are the doctors, healers, physical and mental therapists, coaches, mentors, trainers, self-help gurus, spiritual leaders, and others that we gather into our lives to advise and guide us.

My new friend was in the middle seat of the fully booked Southwest Airlines jet. "Let me tell you my story," she said, and her story was a familiar one that we've all either heard or, too often, experienced. For several months, Julie hadn't quite felt up to par, and had no idea what, if anything was wrong with her. She was a young woman in her late twenties, successful professionally, seemingly in good health, and she was also athletic, playing competitive soccer.

Julie had visited many doctors, and had been given a variety of tests, with the results perplexingly pointing to nothing. Then she heard of Dr. J Dunn. As she told me the story, she gestured a bit with her arms, which she explained was "muscle testing," a process Dr. Dunn performed. "So I went to see Dr. Dunn, who did all kinds of weird stuff," she said. "Dr. Dunn was pushing my arm, while pointing with her fingers at a whole bunch of places on my body. Then, she stopped, and told me one thing: 'I think it would be a good idea if you saw your gynecologist immediately.'"

It turned out that Julie had cervical cancer. Dr. Dunn, without diagnosing it (which is paradoxically against the law unless you are a licensed physician), had found it through her practice of Wholistic Kinesiology.

Dr. Dunn may have saved Julie's life. That was all I had to hear! "Could you please give me Dr. Dunn's phone number," I eagerly asked. The rest is history.

Ten years later, J asked me to write the preface to her wonderful book, which you now have in your hands. I am not a practitioner, I am a client. As are members of my family and my extended family, as are my clients, as well as Olympic athletes, NFL football players, movie stars . . . well, you get the picture. My dogs are clients, too (J has kept one of my sweet Labradors alive long after chemotherapy would have killed him; he has the most aggressive type of fibro sarcoma, yet he keeps chewing on his bones, jumping, running and wagging his tail).

What you have in your hands is the secret formula. I know, because I took J's class, and I can tell you first-hand that she is a genius. One of the very few that I have ever met on this earth. She is a veritable medical encyclopedia on chemistry, biology, nutrition, anatomy . . . you name it. J has kept me healthy through broken bones (football), torn muscles (tennis), flu's, emotional challenges. She has found solutions that have allowed me to circumvent and overcome my own personal travesties and ailments. The magic is not J, the magic is Wholistic Kinesiology. This remarkable system of working with the body to create healing is unprecedented. What Dr. J Dunn has given to all of us is the next great leap forward in this healing paradigm.

I encourage you to delve deeply into the practical applications that you will be trained to master in this book. If you are reading this book, then you likely have a calling in your heart to heal and liberate others and yourself, and to help others live happy, healthy, fulfilled lives. With all of my heart I thank you as I thank J, for sharing this provocative and brilliant work with the world.

—

Mark Weinstein
Author of *Habitually Great.*
www.peaklifehabits.com

ACKNOWLEDGEMENTS

So many people have helped me, instructed me and encouraged me along the way. I appreciate them all so much.

What book on Kinesiology does not have Dr. George Goodheart to thank for his wonderful discovery and unrelenting dedication to the cause of helping human beings become healthier and more in charge of their own lives?

I owe an enormous debt of gratitude to Dr. Stephen Kit Taylor who was and is my mentor, Thank you for giving me the biggest kick in the butt and sending me off to study and always strive to be as good as you.

Thank you Karta Purkh Singh Khalsa and Sewa Singh Khalsa I don't know where I would be without your efforts and incredible knowledge. I feel very fortunate to have been able to study with you.

Thank you Aja Warren for being the biggest inspiration in my life. You gave me the will to turn my life around and begin the healing journey. Daily you help me become a better human being. I can't imagine being blessed with a more amazing daughter and friend than you.

Thank you Mom for inspiring me and always being behind me no matter what. Your faith in me has carried me through many incredibly hard times. Your laughter and joy sing in my heart.

Thank you to my wonderful and incredibly gifted husband, Dr. Glenn Wilcox. You keep me learning, loving, exploring, playing and always searching for more answers to the puzzle of human health. What a joy to share the journey with such a lovely human being and compassionate physician.

Thank you Dwayne "the Rock" Johnson and Dany Garcia for your faith and support in helping me in so many ways to get this book and the institute up and going! I am honored that you saw the potential and benefit that Wholistic Kinesiology is to so many people and gave me such an amazing "leg up" to get the word out!

Dawn Archuleta and Deborah Keller have been the foundation on which the Wholistic Kinesiology Center and Institute depend. None of this would have been possible if they hadn't stood by in me in tough times and continued to believe in the ultimate benefit to so many people. I am so blessed to have such strong women in my life.

Thank you Brenda Robinson for being my patient model!

INTRODUCTION

You can heal your life by listening to your body. I learned this lesson the hard way. But now that I have a greater understanding of health and wellness, I can teach it to you very easily. Just know this: The body remembers everything. The mind may think it can logically explain what's good for you, but the body knows, feels and remembers everything.

Let me explain a little about myself, and how I came to learn so much about how our bodies *really* work. I began my healing journey as many health care practitioners have, by looking for answers to my own health questions. Why was I tired all the time? Why did I hurt all over? Why did I have skull-piercing migraine headaches?

And here's what my body remembered: a bad diet, bad health choices and stresses from my past. As a child, my breakfasts were Pop Tarts, Cap'n Crunch cereal, French toast and the like. Lunches were peanut butter and jelly or bologna sandwiches with milk or Coke. Dinners tended to be processed food. No wonder my teeth were in such bad shape! The dentist plugged my cavities with mercury amalgam fillings – the standard then. And with each new filling, I felt more brain fog, spaciness and fatigue. I was moody and depressed a lot.

The stress of being a teen easily slid into the stress of trying to balance a party-hearty lifestyle with a university education. More stress: I left school after two years and returned home to be with my father, who was dying of lung cancer. After he passed, I lost my desire for college, and drifted west to California. I got into some bad situations and did a lot of drugs. I was on a downhill path to destruction. I got pregnant in 1982 and all partying came to a halt, it was a wakeup call. I married in 1983, the year my daughter was born, then divorced a year later. For the next 10 years, I was a single mom who received little to no child support, bought everything at second-hand stores and worked full time in a bookstore for minimum wage. At night, I painted murals on daycare walls to pay for my daughter's daycare. We did not eat well; McDonalds was our cuisine of choice, and we washed everything down with Cokes and ice tea with NutraSweet.

I began feeling tired all the time. My headaches were becoming more severe. I was nauseous and my joints ached. But I could not go to a doctor – I could not afford health insurance. And I had a child to take care of. Her well being meant more to me than my health. In my mind, I knew I was doing the right thing for her, but my body did not like what I was doing to me. After a year of suffering, I finally broke down and used some money that I was saving up for toys and saw a doctor.

He did blood tests and other exams, said all was normal and gave me a prescription for headaches. I realized then that something was wrong with this scenario. He didn't know what was wrong with me, but was willing to cover up my symptoms with painkillers. I was so frustrated; tears came as easy as breathing. I knew I had to do something, or I would be in no shape to help myself, let alone take care of my daughter.

I decided maybe I was missing some nutrients in my diet. I had read about something like that in a magazine. But which vitamins did I need? I walked into a nearby health food store and was overwhelmed by the shelves stacked floor-to-ceiling with everything from vitamin A to zinc. I talked with a clerk, who listened to my symptoms and suggested that I try chiropractic.

My reply: "Huh? What do fatigue, joint pain and headaches have to do with chiropractors?"

I told my roommate about the clerk's suggestion, and he suggested I try his chiropractor. "He does some very different things, and he's brilliant!" he gushed. I was willing to try anything at this point.

So I visited Dr. Stephen Kit Taylor, a Chiropractor and applied kinesiologist. What a strange experience! He lifted my arm in the air, pushed on it and asked me to resist his push, and poked and prodded various areas of my body. *This is so weird*, I thought. But after a few minutes, he told me my ileocecal valve (the valve that goes from the small intestine to the large intestine) was open, and waste matter was drifting back into my small intestine. That was why I was nauseous, headachy, and hurt all over – my body was being poisoned by my own waste products! Further, I needed to avoid eating raw food, popcorn, caffeine, and spicy foods, which were irritating that area. He gave me adrenal support supplements to increase my energy, and told me to come back in one week to see how I was doing. Intrigued by his findings, I decided to follow his instructions to the tee.

What a difference a week makes! My energy was returning, my mind clearing and my headaches less severe and less often. I saved my money and began visiting Dr. Taylor on a regular basis. His very strange technique of testing my body worked wonders where other doctors had failed. Dr. Taylor also found that I was suffering from a Candida. Candida is a yeast infection, probably from the repeated rounds of antibiotics I had taken in the past for urinary tract infections. He put me on the "Candida" diet, which restricted sugars, yeasts, fermented foods and other items which feed yeast. I began to lose weight and felt great. My brain fog was definitely lifting after many years of living in a mental mist.

It was hard to describe what I was going through to my friends and family, but they all noticed the difference. I told them, "You just have to experience it for yourself," and they did. He became lovingly referred to as "the witch doctor." They made fun of the whole thing, but they all got results. Allergies disappeared, energy returned, aches and pains left; they slept better and many lost weight.

This amazingly simple, yet seemingly mysterious technique made such a profound impression on me that I decided I wanted to learn how to do it myself.

In 1988, I began studying kinesiology when I signed up for a Touch for Health class, a beginner's course that taught muscle testing as a way to learn about musculoskeletal issues. It was fascinating, effective and so much fun. I practiced on family and friends, and they couldn't get enough of it.

My next class – "Brain Gym" – taught me a technique to help balance brain function. Many practitioners use it to help kids with learning disorders and dyslexia. Though my six-year-old daughter had none of these problems, she used "Brain Gym" skills and began getting straight A's in school. And doing some of the mental gymnastics before soccer games even helped her perform better on the soccer field.

In 1990, I had the good fortune to hear about a kinesiology class being taught by Karta Purkh Singh Khalsa, an expert in the field. His technique combined all possible healing modalities into one system. I knew I had to take this course, but I had no money at the time. The $1,500 tuition fee seemed more out of reach than the moon; I was a single mom working at a bookstore for little more than minimum wage, but I knew that somehow I had to take that class. Remarkably, the very next day, my tax return arrived with a refund for exactly $1,500! If this wasn't fate, I didn't know what was.

This new Kinesionics technique was superior to anything I had previously been exposed to. My health began to soar! I still visited Dr. Taylor on occasion, and had to deal with sporadic bouts of Candida (*aargh!*), and needed to stay on the Candida diet. (No sugar, No yeast, No Bread, No Alcohol, No Fun!!) I began seeing a kinesionics practitioner, who was able to completely clear my Candida infection within two weeks. Awesome! I told Dr. Taylor about this new technique of Kinesionics, and he wanted to know more.

I went to his office to show him what I had been learning. I tested him and found a blood sugar imbalance. He was skeptical, so we decided to test his blood sugar with a glucose meter her had. The number was sky high. He was blown away by the accuracy of the testing.

Dr. Taylor was having difficulty with some chronic patients and was looking for more answers. Eventually, he referred one of his clients to me. Carol was a single, tall, beautiful young woman in her early twenties who was wasting away to nothing. For the past several years, she couldn't eat without digestive distress, couldn't go to the bathroom by herself, and had to have enemas or colonics regularly. She had no energy and couldn't work to support herself, so she was forced to live with her abusive parents in a dysfunctional environment.

I was extremely nervous as a new practitioner but felt confident in the technique, so I set aside my fears and agreed to work on her. I realized I had to trust the muscle testing process I had learned and be open to whatever Carol's body told me. I put Carol on her first Kinesionics program and was able to detect underlying health issues, and give her recommendations on nutrients, lifestyle changes, exercise modifications, and dietary choices.

I got a phone call several days later. Carol was ecstatic. Her energy was returning, she could eat without discomfort and, best of all, she had a bowel movement by herself for the first time in years. She cried with joy. I got off the phone and yelled to the world. "*YES!* This is what I want to do for the rest of my life! I want to feel this surge of joy when I help someone regain health! I have never felt anything more rewarding!" Carol eventually regained her health, moved out of her parents' home, and returned to school. Years later, I heard she was married, had a couple of kids and was doing well.

As I began to build a reputation and practice, I knew I needed to learn everything I could about the human body and thought about getting a degree. (Practicing kinesiology does not require a degree in New Mexico, my home.) It had been 10 years since I'd set foot in a college, but I was a different person now. I had drive and motivation, and I knew what path I wanted to walk. I had to follow my inner voice and destiny.

I took a few courses at the local community college in the evenings. Between being a single mother without child support, working full time, practicing on the side and attending classes, it was a full, busy life! But I finished my prerequisites and moved to Davenport, Iowa, to begin chiropractic school in 1991. For the next four years I studied nonstop and barely had time to watch a movie with my daughter. But she was extremely patient and caring, and even helped me study. I graduated in 1995 and moved back home to Albuquerque.

I began to practice with Dr. Taylor, who had introduced me to kinesiology so many years before. It wasn't long before I had a full time practice of my own, using mainly the Kinesionics technique. I wasn't finished learning though. (Hopefully, I never will be.)

In 1996, I opened my own clinic and began teaching part of the Kinesionics six-month course for the Kinesionics Institute. As I learned new techniques, I began developing my own system and in 2000 began teaching what I called "Wholistic Kinesiology" in my clinic. The completeness – the "Wholeness" – seemed to fit. The Wholistic Kinesiology Center, Inc. is now a 5,000-square-foot facility housing a myriad of practitioners who combine kinesiology with the various disciplines they have studied.

Whenever I open the doors at my health center to begin a new day, I re-experience that same joy I felt when I helped my first client find her way back from dis-ease. And then I remember how unhealthy I once was, and how far I have come. It still continues to be a tremendous journey. I learn things daily from the people I work on, by using muscle testing to ask questions of the body.

Now it is time to share their wisdom — and mine — with you.

I hope you enjoy this book, which is filled with healing and self-discovery. My dream is that you will use these techniques for the betterment of mankind. It's time we were given the skills to help each other regain health! The personal touch is such a necessary part of the healing process, and there is more to well-being than just being well.

What you have here is an accumulation of things that I have learned over the years from treating patients, classes that I have taken, books that I have read and suggestions from doctors, clients and from my own intuition. I've tried to give you a great place to start and a thorough understanding of kinesiology, as I know it. Use this book to learn how to read and understand your body. If you need further instruction, the DVD is available and can be extremely helpful, or you can attend our course in person. Because when you know how to read your body, the possibilities for health and wellness are boundless.

Dr. J Dunn

A NOTE ABOUT THIS BOOK

I wrote this book for two reasons: First, for someone who is new to kinesiology, I wanted to present this helpful and life-affirming concept in a simple and easy-to-understand way. Even if you do not have a science background, or if medical terminology tends to bewilder you, have no fears. The ideas you will encounter in the following pages will be clearly explained.

This book is also for the more seasoned practitioner, because there is good, new information here for you, too. This book is the manual I use in the first weekend of the six-month Wholistic Kinesiology course taught at the Wholistic Kinesiology Institute, Inc. in Albuquerque, New Mexico. The first weekend and the entire course is also available on DVD and is designed to be studied at home. See our Web site www.wholistickinesiology.com for more information.

However, please realize that the information contained in this instruction manual is not intended to diagnose or treat illness or disease, or replace the services of a professional, licensed healthcare practitioner. The ultimate responsibility for treatment rests with you. If you have a serious medical condition, please consult a licensed physician or therapist. Working toward healing yourself is very admirable, but please realize that some may need the help of a trained professional. Neither the author nor the publisher can be held responsible for any consequences arising from the use of the information contained in this manual.

PART I

WHAT IS WHOLISTIC KINESIOLOGY?

CHAPTER 1
THE BODY-MIND RELATIONSHIP

I recently observed an exercise class at a health club, and watched several dozen men and women of all ages lying on their backs on the floor doing leg lifts. "Raise those quads!" encouraged the peppy, young teacher at the front of the room. "Flex those glutes!" she energetically called, her auburn ponytail bobbing while she waved her fists. And then she said, "If you don't take care of your body, your body won't take care of you!"

I paused to think about those words for a moment, and realized that the teacher's well-intentioned sentiments were only half right. Actually, your body will always do its best to take care of you. Always. And, furthermore, your body always knows what's best for you.

And that, in a nutshell, is the basis of kinesiology. Your body always knows what's best for you. Keep that axiom in mind as you read this book, and I guarantee the concepts you will encounter will be as clear as a mountain lake at sunrise.

To reiterate: Your body will always do its best to take care of you. However, unfortunately, not everyone does their best to take care of their body. They feed their body with junk food, or processed chow from a can, and never pass on a tempting sugary dessert. Furthermore, they skimp on eating fruits and vegetables. They work long hours without breaks, don't get adequate sleep and surround themselves with negative people and situations.

Think of it this way: You wouldn't fill the gas tank in your car with water and expect to get peak performance, would you? But yet there are some people who keep gassing up with the cheapest fuel imaginable, then act surprised when they start hearing pinging or knocking in the engine. That's the car's way of telling you, "This junk you're putting inside me isn't good for my metal health." And guess what happens? The car stalls out somewhere. And then there you are at the side of the road, your hood up, waiting for the Triple-A guy (or gal), and wishing you would have paid more attention when your car first started making rattling noises.

In the same way that your car "talks" to you, your body talks to you. For example, when you get headaches, it means something. No one gets headaches for no reason. Instead of just popping a few aspirins and trying to wish your headache would go away, why not listen to your body? Is your body trying to tell you that you are putting too much sugar, soda pop or other cheap fuels into your body? Or maybe is your monitor screen too bright? Do your glasses need cleaning? Maybe there is an ingredient in your cologne or perfume that is not reacting well with you.

Or perhaps that headache is a symptom of something deeper, more physiological. Do these sudden, blinding headaches seem to sear the insides of your eyeballs? It's time to pay attention!

Suffering from a stomachache? Better look at your diet — what are you eating that's upsetting you? Or perhaps your body is giving you a message: What is it about your life that you cannot "stomach"?

Back pain? Are you lifting more than you can handle, or did you not warm up before going out to shovel snow? Or, at a deeper level, is your body trying to tell you that you need more "spine" because you should stand up for yourself more often?

Our body is wise, and can tell us so much. But in this first book, I want to concentrate more on the physical aspect of our body, and not so much on the psychological and emotional messages our body can give. In the extended portion of the course we delve into this subject in great detail.

Let me return a moment to the health club I was observing. After the exercise class, I stuck around to watch a yoga class. As the teacher demonstrated "the swan," which involves tucking one leg under the torso while stretching the arms forward, she gently told her class, "Listen to your body. Yoga is not a competition with yourself. If your knees begin to hurt, stop and go to a softer position."

Good teacher! Gold star for her!

THE NATURAL ABILITY TO HEAL

Here is another axiom to keep in mind when trying to understand kinesiology: Your body has the remarkable gift to be able to repair itself. And this all happens unconsciously. Remember your last paper cut? You did not have to stare at your fingertip and send healing thoughts to your skin. No, you just washed off the cut, maybe put a Band-Aid on it, then went on with your life. And a few days later, not even a scar remained – it was as if you had never cut yourself at all!

"Your body will work hard on its own to help you recover – even if you do little to help the process along," says physiatrist (a doctor of physical medicine and rehabilitation) Julie K. Silver, M.D., in an article in *AARP: The Magazine*. Dr. Silver explains how, biologically, our bodies are self-programmed to control infection while promoting healing, no matter the injury. Whether we suffer through a disease, a pulled muscle or a broken bone, our body has the natural ability to want to heal itself.

Let me repeat the key words in that sentence: "want to". Our body has no choice but to want to heal itself. (Except in a few extreme cases, where physiological problems come into play.) Your body wants to run at its optimal condition. But, how do we know what the body is saying?

Dr. Silver says there are three fundamentals that will put people on the path to optimal healing:

- **Don't Neglect Nutrition** – Vitamins, carbohydrates and a colorful array of fruits and vegetables are critical to a healing diet.
- **Make Sleep a Priority** – During an illness, you need more than seven to eight hours of sleep a night.
- **Get Yourself Moving** – Exercise helps us heal faster.

Seems simple enough, right? The problem is, sometimes, life gets in the way. People eat on the go, sleep when they can, and exercise – who has time for that? Unfortunately, some people let life get in the way too much, and then the life of ease turns into dis-ease, and it is time to visit the doctor.

Suppose you felt ill and went to the doctor. Your physician would run some tests and make his or her best diagnosis. And, being a good patient, you would totally accept what the doctor said. Even if a little voice in the back of your mind thought, *This just doesn't feel right...*

Or suppose the doctor plainly asked you, "What kind of medicine is best for you?" or "Why kind of therapy should I prescribe?" You can not answer that, of course; if you are not a doctor. Your mind can not answer that either — it is too busy thinking about what type of medicines your health plan will cover, how a few days sick from work will screw up your schedule, who will take care of your family should you become unwell, and so forth.

Your mind may not know what is best for you, but your body knows. That is the essence of kinesiology. And that is what I will teach you in this book: How to listen to your body. Understanding the relationship between you and your body is what kinesiology is all about.

Remember:

      * Your body always knows what's best for you.
      * Your body will always do its best to take care of you.
      * If you take care of your body, your body will be healthy.

CHAPTER 2
UNDERSTANDING KINESIOLOGY

Kinesiology is the study of the movement of body parts, and a kinesiologist is trained to evaluate and treat muscular imbalances and other problems of the musculoskeletal system. Kinesiology combines human anatomy, physiology, biomechanics, exercise physiology, exercise psychology and sociology, history, and philosophy of sport. Or, put simply, kinesiology explores the relationship between the quality of movement and overall human health.

Wholistic Kinesiology is regarded as a clinical use of the science of Kinesiology. It is both an art form and a science. It is regarded as a science because it has rules, methods, principles and logical techniques; it is also an art form, because it also involves intuitions, feelings and practice.

Wholistic Kinesiology uses a muscle testing system to "speak to" and get information from the body. This information can deal with a person's nutritional, physical and/or emotional health. Briefly, muscle testing involves placing a part of the body in a specific position, and then applying pressure to that body part or body area. When pressure is applied to an area of the skin – which covers the muscles – signals are sent via the nerve endings in that section of skin through the muscles to the central processing centers in the brain, which register sensations. If the body is healthy, the muscles remain strong, but if a problem is detected in the circuit, the muscles will display negative energy and weaken temporarily. Therefore, whether the muscle either holds fast or gives in to the pressure will let the kinesiologist know if there is a problem to be addressed.

Here is another way to look at how our muscle system works with our emotional well-being: Think of a polygraph ("lie detector test"). Polygraphs identify a person's physiological reaction by detecting when negative behavior is being displayed. As a person is questioned about a certain topic, fluctuations in the person's heart rate, respiratory rate, blood pressure, and even a change in the amount of sweat excreted may indicate if the person being tested is being deceptive.

Remember the "lie detector game" you played as a child? Fill a bowl with water, then stick your finger in the water. Have a friend ask you a series of questions, and try to lie on some of the answers. Notice how whenever you fib, your finger moves and makes ripples in the water.

Wholistic Kinesiology uses this same body-emotion-mind principle. The beauty of Wholistic Kinesiology is that it allows your practitioner to test for the best possible healing path for you to take.

Later in this book, I will describe in more full terms the art and science behind Wholistic Kinesiology, and how I used kinesiological principles to develop this system. I will also present exercises you can do to learn to master Wholistic Kinesiology. But first, let's try another simple exercise to demonstrate muscle testing, and test this hypothesis I proposed in the previous chapter.

YOUR BODY ALWAYS KNOWS WHAT'S BEST FOR YOU.

Have you ever been in a supermarket, and as you were walking down the produce aisle, suddenly felt compelled to buy an item? (No, I'm not talking about the chocolate bar that looked pretty good — however, after ovulation, women are often drawn to dark chocolate, which is full of magnesium, a mineral that the body loses during menstruation.) This is your body talking to you, saying it needs a certain vitamin or mineral that is found in that fruit or vegetable.

So, here is a simple way to see if, let's say, you should be taking more of a certain vitamin. Go to your local health food store, or to the supplement section of a nearby drugstore. Pick up a bottle of Vitamin A and hold it to your stomach. Close your eyes, and try to clear your mind. Then think to yourself: Do I need to add more Vitamin A to my diet? If yes, I will lean slightly forward. If I need less Vitamin A, I will tilt backward. If I am fine, I will not move. Then, notice how your body moves. Repeat this action for other vitamins, minerals and supplements — B, C, D, E, zinc, evening primrose, saw palmetto, etc. You may be surprised by what you may be lacking in your diet! (If you have any questions or concerns about the results you obtain, please consult a licensed nutritionist.)

By the way, if you are a tad on the shy side, I recommend doing this exercise in a health food store, where sales clerks are used to seeing people muscle test products all the time, and probably will not give you a strange look.

THE HISTORY OF KINESIOLOGY

George Goodheart Jr., D.C., one of the founders of modern kinesiology, wrote this very succinct description of how kinesiology works. He stated:

"The body heals itself by primary intent. It heals itself in a sure, sensible, practical, reasonable, and observable manner. The healer within can be approached from without. Man possesses a potential for recovery through the ... innate intelligence of the human structure. This recovery potential, with which he has been naturally endowed, and which is his natural birthright, merely waits for the trained hand, the knowing mind, and the caring heart of the trained individual to bring it to physical manifestation, allowing health to come forth.... It allows the same force which created the body to heal the body and allow it to operate unimpeded."

Though Dr. Goodheart is credited as a leader in developing Applied Kinesiology, the ideas behind this therapeutic system have been around for quite awhile. Aristotle, who lived in ancient Greece, is often called "the father of kinesiology" because he wrote *Parts of Animals, Movement of Animals* and *Progression of Animals*, which described muscle action in terms of geometric analysis. Archimedes and, later in Rome, Galen wrote discourses on how muscular activity impacted the body. In the 15th century, Leonardo de Vinci, who was fascinated by human anatomy, intuited that muscles somehow interacted with nerves to cause motion.

Kinesiology, as a system involving muscle manipulation, was first explored in 1932 by R.W Lovett, an orthopedic surgeon, and later by osteopath Frank Chapman, who discovered that poor lymph flow was the result of some diseases. Chapman found that rubbing areas of the lymphatic system which were tender could improve certain conditions. Terence Bennet, another chiropractor, determined that improving the blood flow also helped alleviate certain conditions. He devised a system of monitor points on the body, which led to the neurovascular points system used today. (For a more complete explanation of monitor points, see Chapter 3.)

In 1964, Goodheart discovered an amazing connection between weak muscles and organ imbalances. He observed identical organ or gland problems in several patients who had the same muscle weakness. He then began to make a list linking specific muscles with specific organs and glands. The first association he discovered was between the shoulder muscles and the stomach. When he was able to correct (strengthen) weak muscles through various exercise techniques, the associated organs began to function better. He deduced the following:

- Specific health problems may cause specific muscles to test weak.
- The muscle that tests weak due to a health problem can be used as an indicator to determine possible treatments of that health problem.
- Treatments making the muscle test strong may positively influence the health problem. So, balancing the muscle helps the organ, and balancing the organ through nutrients can also strengthen the muscle.

Goodheart also found that using a system known in Chinese medicine as meridian points (which are used in acupuncture) provided him with another set of corrections which could be used during diagnosis and treatment. He named this new system Applied Kinesiology, and it is still used today by chiropractors.

In 1970, John Thie, D.C., an early student and research partner of Goodheart's, wanted to make Applied Kinesiology available to the general public, while Goodheart thought Applied Kinesiology should only be taught to professionals. Goodheart challenged Thie to write an easy-to-understand how-to manual if he truly wanted to achieve his goal and in 1973, John Thie published *Touch for Health*. The book contains a simplified discussion of Applied Kinesiology for lay people who desired to understand the techniques and pass them on to others and share this gift of healing.

Touch for Health has since been translated into 24 languages and has been taught in over 100 countries. We have incorporated the "Touch for Health" methods to evaluate individual muscle strength in the Wholistic Kinesiology technique, which we will discuss in the next book.

CHAPTER 3
PRINCIPLES OF APPLIED KINESIOLOGY

Allopathic — "traditional" or "conventional" — medicine believes in trying to outsmart the body. Doctors who practice allopathic medicine believe that disease occurs because the body has made a mistake. Traditional physicians pay attention to the symptoms of the disease, and often prescribe medicine aimed at curing an illness while making the patient comfortable. Furthermore, many allopathic doctors believe in the germ theory — infectious diseases result from the action of microorganisms — instead of seeing disease as a signal of some kind of imbalance in the body.

Natural medicine instead tries to use the healing power inherent in nature to stimulate the organism's healing process. Examples of natural medicine include homeopathy, chiropractic, acupuncture, naturopathy, hydrotherapy, massage therapy, and nutritional/lifestyle practices.

Somewhere between natural and allopathic medicine are "alternative," "complementary" or "integrative" medicine, which link the two in a "best of both worlds" manner.

THE DIFFERENCES BETWEEN ALLOPATHIC AND NATURAL MEDICINE

ALLOPATHIC MEDICINE

Believes in trying to outsmart the body.
The body is making a mistake and we must correct it.
Treats symptoms instead of causes.
Believes in the germ theory.
Specializes in emergency medicine

<u>Wholistic (Natural or Alternative) Medicine</u>

Believes in inherent wisdom of the body
Tries to get to the root of the health problem
Believes in balance of the terrain
Specializes in preventive medicine

HOW KINESIOLOGY WORKS

Because kinesiology is a relatively new system of treatment, many in the established medical community think of it as complementary or alternative medicine, something to be tried as a last resort, or they lump it together with acupuncture, reflexology, aromatherapy and the like. Others, unfortunately, dismiss kinesiology as "New Agey", a fad, or something downright mystical that should be avoided at all costs.

When you think about it, this "modern" method of medicine is actually quite old. As we saw in the last chapter, even Aristotle and Archimedes were exploring the relationship between our muscles and our physical well-being.

Today, kinesiological information is used in such fields as physical therapy, occupational therapy, chiropractic, osteopathy, kinesiotherapy, massage therapy, ergonomics, physical education and athletic coaching. The approach of these applications can be therapeutic, preventive, or high-performance. Kinesiology also incorporates knowledge from other academic disciplines such as psychology, physiology, sociology, cultural studies, ecology, evolutionary biology, and anthropology. Kinesiology is also related to other fields that combine motor skills and dexterity research, such as graphonomics – the study of handwriting movement control – and the study of motor control in speech.

Some professional physical therapists are also fully credentialed as "Registered Kinesiologists." The general difference between the job of a kinesiologist and a physical therapist is that a kinesiologist will assess movement, or problems in movement with regard to physiology, anatomy and biomechanics, while a physical therapist will actually assess and apply therapeutic techniques to correct motor skills problems.

MUSCLE TESTING

Muscle testing had already been accepted as a valid technique to evaluate the neurological function of a muscle when Dr. George Goodheart began using muscle testing in his chiropractic practice in 1964. Indeed, neurology textbooks of the time included discussions of muscle testing, defining it as "a means of testing the motor function of limbs." Goodheart later refined muscle testing by linking muscles to the body's energy system, as employed in acupuncture. This became the basis of the system that was known as Applied Kinesiology.

One of the ideas behind Goodheart's theory of Applied Kinesiology deals with how he envisioned the various systems of the body working together. Goodheart formulated what he called the "triad of health" — three equal facets of human development that depended and supported each other. When the triad was balanced, the result was total wellness.

His triad included:

- Structural (body)
- Emotional (mind)
- Biochemical (energy)

Energy refers to the fuel that powers the body. Think of your body as a miniature power plant that supplies energy every moment to the dozens of bioelectric processes that are always at work: nerves communicate sensations to your brain, your autonomic nervous system keeps your heart charged so it pumps continuously, your brain creates holographic memories from stored bits of intelligence that can be accessed at lightening speed so you can read these words, connect the ideas and their meanings make sense to you. But I am going to also take this notion one step further — energy is not just the fuel that runs your body, it includes the nutrients you take into your body so your digestive system can create the best fuel to keep your body from blowing fuses, and make sure your miniature power plant never breaks down.

THERAPY LOCALIZATION

Even though the Applied Kinesiology triad linked structure/neurological, chemical/nutrition, and mental/emotional aspects of health, as well as adding into the mix several western and eastern healing methods (like acupuncture), Goodheart was still faced with questions about how reliable the system could be in terms of diagnoses.

- First, how can someone using this technique determine what should be treated first? Without a priority, one would need to treat all three sides of the Triad equally each time.
- Second, how can one treat problems with no known muscle association?

While puzzling out these problems, Goodheart discovered a procedure called "therapy localization." Under this procedure, the therapist simply touches the body in a specific area and tests a strong muscle. If it weakens, then the area of contact is a problem area, or is connected to a problem area.

However, therapy localization only revealed the location of the problem, not what the problem was. While therapy localization was a good start to point physicians in the right direction, further research was needed to determine which type of therapy would be most effective to treat that problem.

MONITOR POINTS

Monitor points (also called therapy localization points and acupuncture indicator points) are locations on the surface of the body that correspond to imbalances found within the body. They are used to monitor the functioning of organ systems or nutrient levels used to power those systems.

Acupuncturists use these points to reduce pain in a patient when they place their needles along meridians – paths of energy flow throughout the body – to balance energy flow.

In fact, many of the points we use in kinesiology have their origins in acupuncture. Along the meridians there are various points that come close to the surface of the body and can be useful in diagnosis and treatment of certain problems. We call these alarm points.

In the 1930's, osteopath Frank Chapman, D.C., developed a system of reflex point massage to increase the lymphatic drainage of particular organs and glands. Goodheart experimented with these "Chapman Reflexes" and found that many of them strengthened previously weak testing muscles. These reflexes have since become known as neurolymphatic reflexes.

Also in the 1930's, chiropractor Terrence Bennett, D.C., found that when he touched certain points on the skin, the blood flow to specific organs increased. This increased flow balanced out organ functions. Dr. Bennett spent hundreds of hours touching various points on patients' skin and scalp, and observing the resultant reactions of their organs under an x-ray fluoroscope. Goodheart found that stimulating these spots on the skin also strengthened weak testing muscles, and he began incorporating this practice into his system. These points later became known as neurovascular reflexes.

Let me simplify things a bit. Rather than try to keep track of all these various touching points and reflexes, just be aware that all of these discoveries and more are utilized in the Wholistic Kinesiology system of evaluation. We have used these testing points successfully for many years. And when new methods of diagnosis are found that are proved to be useful for monitoring function in the body, that information, too, is assimilated into the ever-expanding database that is Wholistic Kinesiology. (A more full explanation of Wholistic Kinesiology will be found in Chapter 4.)

HAND MODES

Dr. Alan Beardall, one of Goodheart's students, began using Applied Kinesiology in a different way. He created the therapeutic system called Clinical Kinesiology.

Beardall's method involved developing a dialogue with the patient's subconscious. This was especially helpful for patients who had dealt with longtime unresolved physical problems, as well as emotional problems that manifested themselves in the body as physical problems. Other patients had ignored ailments and then, over time, developed compensating behaviors – for example, someone with a hip pain issue began limping, then adapted to the limp when the hip no longer was causing pain. Clinical Kinesiology allowed the body to penetrate the adaptive patterns to disclose the underlying problem that needed treatment.

Beardall discovered hand modes quite by accident. During a treatment session, he had found a weak muscle, he left the patient for a moment to document that finding in the patient's file. When he, moments later, retested the muscle for confirmation, the muscle seemed to have grown strong on its own. While attempting to discover how this could have happened, Beardall noticed that the patient had several fingers touching each other. Retesting with the hand opened resulted in the original weak muscle. Fingers touching equaled strong muscle; hand open equaled weak muscle. This simple serendipitous discovery led to the development of hundreds of mudras (hand modes) to clarify and evaluate the body's problems and find the best solutions.

Beardall's hand modes allowed the practitioner to get specific information from the nervous system, and are a great tool for getting to deeper layers of imbalance in the body. With this technique, a practitioner could literally, through the patient's hand, "ask" the body where the problem was, and if it needed emotional work, better nutrition or bodywork to correct it. (A demonstration of this method will be found in Part III.)

KINESIONICS

Karta Purkh Singh Khalsa developed Kinesionics after studying with Dr. Beardall. He simplified Beardall's techniques and added new therapy localization points and new ways to evaluate levels of imbalance. His system was much easier to learn and use and was taught for the first time to lay persons.

I began studying with Karta Purkh after I had learned the Touch for Health system, Behavioral Kinesiology and Brain Gym systems of Kinesiology, and found the technique to be very comprehensive and easy to use. Where some systems concentrated only on one aspect of healing, Karta Purkh developed a framework for incorporating many healing modalities into one treatment method.

I had been teaching and practicing the Kinesionics technique all through Chiropractic school, but in 1996 I opened my own clinic and started teaching part of the Kinesionics six-month course for the Kinesionics Institute. As I began to learn new and different techniques, I realized that I needed to develop my own method of diagnosis and treatment, which would be a combination of all the techniques I had learned and the information I was gathering through private practice. In 2000, I began teaching "Wholistic Kinesiology", a modern synthesis of Western and Eastern medicine. I liked the spelling of Holistic with a "W". It was the completeness or "Wholeness" of the technique that seemed to fit.

My clinic has since grown to 5,000 square feet, and we have a large variety of practitioners. All of them combine kinesiology with the various disciplines they have studied. The Wholistic Kinesiology Center, Inc. has colon therapists that test to see if a colonic would be beneficial for you, what ingredients to add in at the end (no pun intended!), how often to do it, etc. Our physicians can test patients for the right medication (if it is absolutely necessary), or test them for lifestyle changes such as change of diet. Some of our practitioners specialize in emotional balancing and use muscle testing to determine limiting underlying beliefs that get in the way of success in life. We have estheticians that test for the right beauty products and ingredients of the facials they give. I use kinesiology when I adjust a patient to determine the exact area of subluxation (misalignment) and which direction of correction is best. We have acupuncturists that combine muscle testing with their disciplines. This all serves to make each one of these practices that much more efficient and effective.

Here is my motto:

With the knowledge each individual possesses, combined with direct feedback from the body, the possibilities are unlimited.

A NEW UNDERSTANDING

While drugs, surgery and hospitals have improved our life expectancy in emergency situations, they are not always the answer to chronic health problems. I believe enhancing the natural healing capacity of the body is the key to wellness and a healthful life. Improving the diet, emotions, exercise and lifestyle are the building blocks of healing.

It's encouraging to see that traditional doctors are beginning to respond to the demands of consumers for more natural health care solutions. Nutrition and other alternative and integrative practices have in the past been strictly elective courses for physicians, and not much in the way of natural medicine was taught to them in medical school. Instead, it had to be studied outside of the university.

Today, many medical schools are including an integrative medical program, and more and more physicians are attending nutritional conferences. This is a very exciting development. I recently attended a seminar on "Functional Medicine" in Vancouver, British Columbia, Canada, where over 600 doctors were in attendance. The majority were M.D.'s. I was encouraged.

It is in the spirit of looking forward that I created Wholistic Kinesiology. The system combines the natural disciplines of chiropractic, acupuncture, nutrition, manual muscle testing and Applied Kinesiology. In addition, we have added techniques such as Emotional Freedom Technique, Allergy Elimination and many other cutting-edge therapies. The science of Wholistic Kinesiology is a collection of diagnostic tools and treatment techniques, and each practitioner adds or eliminates information as new ideas arise. As a result, Wholistic Kinesiology must be considered a work in progress. You, hopefully, will take what you learn here and expand it even further, or take it and adapt it to what works best for you and your clients.

CHAPTER 4
WHOLISTIC KINESIOLOGY

What if you had an alarm signal that beeped every time you tried a supplement or food that was bad for you? This would be very handy to direct you toward optimal health. The truth is that we do have this alarm. Sleepiness, mental fog, aches and pains, slight headache and intestinal pain are all alarms that something is wrong in the body. Unfortunately, we have become so adept at living with the alarms, we no longer hear them. But if we listened closely to the signals our body gave us, we would have no problems knowing when to seek help. Thankfully, muscle testing allows us to listen to our body's signals again, and tap into the information our body gives us in a very gentle manner.

If we paid attention to what our bodies were trying to say and only did healthful practices the majority of the time, we would have radiant health way beyond our wildest dreams. We would live to be more than 100 years old, have sex lives that would make Hugh Hefner envious and be resistant to disease processes. The power of natural medicine is that we believe in the inherent wisdom of the body. If we listened to what our body was saying, we would get to the root of any health problem and prevent it from becoming a much bigger crisis.

Modern medicine has little to offer in this regard, except some vague advice about balanced diet, getting some exercise and avoiding stress. (If it were only that simple!!) It is easy to get lost in one-size-fits-all diets, health books and supplement routines. But how can you find the exact diet and supplement program for you in a book written about someone else? Can some author, whom you have never met, guarantee that a low-carb diet is the key to your wellness?

Kinesiology is a modality whose time has come. Why? Because only your unique, individual body can give you personalized feedback in the way that your own health can be restored. We all have very different needs. We have different genetic makeup, eat different diets, enjoy different lifestyles and experience differing stress levels; therefore, it stands to reason that our nutrient needs would vary. Therefore, you can get very specific about how to heal your life by using Wholistic Kinesiology.

PRINCIPLES OF WHOLISTIC KINESIOLOGY

Wholistic Kinesiology is different than kinesiology in that Wholistic Kinesiology is used in a clinical setting to evaluate much more than muscle strength. Put simply, *It is the art and science of neuromuscular evaluation for optimizing health.* If we want to get more complicated, Wholistic Kinesiology is a neurological test for speaking to the body, evaluating the body's electromagnetic potentials. Or put it this way: Wholistic Kinesiology helps you get in touch with your inner power plant.

Wholistic Kinesiology works with the nervous system, which is an electrical system that has positive and negative flows. Our body creates a very measurable electromagnetic field around it, and this field can be shorted out just like our electrical systems in our homes. Think of it this way: How many times have you heard someone who has gotten very angry say, "I've just blown a fuse"?

Wholistic Kinesiology also makes great use of the Chinese systems of meridians, the pathways in the body through which our energy flows. The eastern medical practitioners have paved the way for us by literally mapping out these electrical highways in the body. If electrical energy is not flowing properly to an organ or muscle or joint, we can detect this imbalance through testing the nervous system. This system of diagnosis may sound simplistic, but it is very profound and valuable. We can literally ask the body how things are going internally.

When we see signs of imbalance by looking at someone, such as fatigue, paleness, weak nails, dark circles under the eyes and so forth, we can interpret these as signs that the body is trying to tell us something. If we cover them up we only mask the signs and ignore the cause. With kinesiology, we can use the signs to get to the root of a problem. We can also detect imbalances before they become symptomatic; in fact, I have countless times told patients what was going on in their body before they even knew or felt the symptoms.

THE BASIC TENANTS OF WHOLISTIC KINESIOLOGY:

I.   The body has an amazing ability to be well if it is given the right tools. The power that made the body can heal the body.

2.   The body can tell you through muscle testing where imbalances are.

3.   The body runs on food, (carbohydrates, proteins, fats), vitamins and minerals, and if it gets the proper amounts of these nutrients, it will run smoothly and you will be healthy. If you ignore any of these elements, your body will begin to malfunction and disease may begin.

4.   Lack of the above nutrients can come from variety of sources: A poor diet, improper use of supplements, excess stress (emotional, physical and chemical), lack of exercise, active disease processes, (parasites, yeast or fungal infections, viruses), toxicity and hereditary factors.

5.   The body can tell you what it needs through muscle testing and how much of some curative factor it needs in a very accurate way.

I know that this sounds way too simple and easy. And it is! I have seen these techniques work miracles over and over again in the many years that I have been using Kinesiology. The power and beauty of the human body still constantly amazes me. It is truly a miraculous system. And I am amazed at how well these techniques work at helping to restore the body back to balance and health. I see people get their lives back daily. It works for everyone!

OTHER TECHNIQUES IN WHOLISTIC KINESIOLOGY

When I developed Wholistic Kinesiology, I incorporated only the best and most powerful healing techniques I had learned and used through the years. Some of these disciplines include chiropractic, physiotherapy, massage, clinical nutrition, orthomolecular medicine, herbal medicine, homeopathy, acupuncture, acupressure, emotional counseling, Bach flower remedies, essential oils, allergy desensitization, and so much more.

I now teach this course throughout the World. Wholistic Kinesiology continues to be improved and updated as the class goes on and new healing discoveries occur. Many brilliant minds are combining to create the most powerful healing system available.

The following are techniques that I have studied through the years and that have contributed to the evolution of Wholistic Kinesiology:

- **Applied Kinesiology** – A procedure developed by Dr. George Goodheart that presumes illnesses are the result of improperly balanced energy fields in the body.
- **Clinical Kinesiology** – A procedure developed by Dr. Alan Beardall that focuses on the biological health of a patient.
- **Touch for Health** – A simplified method of Applied Kinesiology developed by Dr. John Thie.
- **Kinesionics** – A muscle testing practice developed by Karta Purkh Singh Khalsa that uses a patient's nervous system to learn about their physical and mental health.
- **Reflexology and acupressure techniques** – Helps relieve muscle strain and improve nerve flow to the organs.
- **Muscle Balancing** – A treatment system developed by Karta Purkh Singh Khalsa that helps patients maintain a healthy muscle response.
- **Meridian Balancing** – A system developed by Karta Purkh Singh Khalsa that desensitizes the body to potentially allergic substances.
- **Brimhall Technique** – A diagnostic system developed by Dr. John Brimhall that combines muscle testing and chiropractic.
- **Contact Reflex Analysis** – A diagnostic system developed by Dr. Versandahl that uses monitor points on the body.
- **Brain Gym** – A form of educational kinesiology that is useful for balancing the hemispheres of the brain.
- **Nambudripod Allergy Elimination Technique (NAET)** – A system developed by Dr. Devi Nambudripod to desensitize persons to allergic substances.

- **Injury Recall Technique** – A method that seeks to heal neurological scars caused by physical injuries developed by Dr. Walter Schmidt and Dr. George Goodheart.
- **Emotional Freedom Technique** – A method developed by Gary Craig to help balance emotional issues and phobias that are held in the body's emotions.
- **Neuro-linguistic Programming** – A procedure developed by Richard Bandler and John Grinder that links how we think and communicate with how our emotions affect our behavior.
- **Shock Release** – A procedure developed by Dr. John Brimhall to release emotional trauma.
- **Feelings Buried Alive** – A system developed by Karol Truman that explores how deep-seated emotions affect the body.
- **Neuro Emotional Technique (NET)** – A system developed by Dr. Scott Walker to pinpoint past emotional issues and alleviate stress in the body.

Now, that you have a good understanding of Wholistic Kinesiology, let's see how this system actually works.

PART II

HOW DOES WHOLISTIC KINESIOLOGY WORK?

Here are a few examples that demonstrate how Wholistic Kinesiology was used to determine the underlying causes of physical symptoms. In Part III, I will present specific exercises that were used to find these ailments, and then used to plan a course of action to help the patient find wellness. But first, I think it is a good idea to present, using real-world stories, how Wholistic Kinesiology works.

Each of the following case studies is based on a real situation and an authentic medical issue. However, to protect the client's privacy, I have changed their names and altered some the non-essential details.

PSUEDOTUMOR CEREBRI ("FALSE BRAIN TUMOR")

Adrian was a 25-year-old beautiful, raven-haired woman who was a successful businesswoman with many friends and an active social life. To her friends, associates and co-workers, Adrian seemed to live life as if every day was her birthday. Unfortunately, in her heart of hearts, she was miserable. She was overweight, often felt too tired to get up from her couch at the end of the day, and she was suffering in silence from constant jaw and face pain, and severe migraine headaches. In addition, she was having two periods a month, and both were extremely painful and heavy. Plus, she suffered from insomnia, allergies and memory loss.

I tested Adrian using the Wholistic Kinesiology prioritization system, and her body showed imbalances in the pituitary, thyroid and ovary reflex points. These are points on the body that are used to evaluate the relative functioning of the endocrine system. When touching these points and testing using the indicator muscle as a feedback system, we determined that these areas were out of balance. After all, muscle testing can sort out exactly where the body needs to begin the healing process! I put Adrian on some supplements that we muscle tested together, and determined what she should take to strengthen her imbalances. (Incidentally, we only use all natural supplements – vitamins, minerals, herbs, homeopathics or dietary changes – to balance health issues.)

Adrian returned 27 days later and reported that she had only had one headache that month, and only had one period, which was much less painful – there was no breakthrough bleeding. Also, her jaw pain was gone, she was sleeping better and she had no allergy symptoms. She was feeling much better overall.

I didn't see Adrian again for two years. Unfortunately, during that time, she had stopped taking her supplements and went back to eating an unhealthy diet (mostly fast food and very little fruits or vegetables). Needless to say, all her symptoms returned and were much worse. She sought help from an M.D., and his recommendations terrified her more than the symptoms she was exhibiting.

Her physician performed blood tests, took an MRI of the brain and gave her a spinal tap to try to determine the source of her severe headaches and hormonal imbalance. She even underwent an optical exam to find out the source of increased pressure in her eyes. After waiting on pins and needles for about a week for the test results, Adrian's physician called her in for a grim-faced consultation.

There were some minor irregularities in Adrian's blood work, and salivary hormonal tests pointed to an imbalance in the pituitary gland (the part of the brain that regulates the body's hormonal levels) but, overall, the doctors were stumped as to the cause of Adrian's symptoms. Their best-guess diagnosis was pseudotumor cerebri (false brain tumor), which is fluid buildup in the brain that results in increased pressure in the cranium. The condition is most common in women between the ages of 20 and 50, and treatment involves removing excess fluid through spinal taps or surgery. Steroids are often prescribed to reduce swelling in the brain tissue. Adrian's physician prescribed a drug called Diamox to reduce the production of cerebral spinal fluid and told her the next resort was to drill through her head to relieve pressure and prevent blindness.

Shaken by the test results, Adrian returned to me for advice. She remembered how the only relief she had ever gotten from her problems was through the Wholistic Kinesiology technique. I retested her and found her progesterone levels were extremely low, and recommended she take natural progesterone.

She returned a few months later for her next visit and reported that all migraines were gone, her period was once again normal and she was feeling great. She was losing weight and her energy was higher than ever. She had discontinued taking Diamox and, better than that, was finally able to laugh at the idea of getting a hole in the head.

She continues to be treated with Wholistic Kinesiology on a regular basis and has had no return of the migraines or symptoms of pseudotumor cerebri.

Adrian's case pretty much typifies the successes I have found using Wholistic Kinesiology. I love rereading my patients' stories, because they prove that the body obviously knows what it needs to regain its sense of balance. Adrian's body was smart enough to know what it required, and it clearly indicated that point through the muscle testing. And what is best of all: Adrian and I were able to totally resolve her symptoms using natural methods, without covering up her dis-ease with medications, which often have harmful side effects.

SEVERE ARTHRITIS AND OSTEOPOROSIS

Suzanne was an 84-year-old woman who loved being surrounded by people. Her eyes were filled with wisdom and light, and her infectious laugh was the result of a great sense of humor. Suzanne had been a music teacher to hundreds of children in her life, and she loved playing the piano. Suzanne had never married, music was her love and her life. Sadly, though, she'd had to stop playing because of the pain in her joints and a severe fatigue that she could not seem to chase away. She also complained of bouts of diverticulitis – an intestinal inflammation – which led to bowel impactions that required hospitalization. In addition her blood pressure was high at 150/80 – normal is 120/80 – and she was taking blood pressure medication and a diuretic to control it. Furthermore, Suzanne was experiencing severe hair loss, and she seemed to have lost the senses of taste and smell. She was regularly sick with the flu, which often turned to pneumonia. She had severe pain in the hip joint, which her M.D. said would require hip replacement surgery. She had also been on Synthroid – a thyroid medication – since age 24. But her blood work looked normal, so her M.D.s didn't suspect a problem.

I evaluated Suzanne using Wholistic Kinesiology and was able to easily determine where the imbalances were in her body. Despite the fact that she was taking medication to increase her hormone production, the Synthroid was not converting into an active thyroid hormone. She was low in zinc and selenium, which was keeping her metabolism from converting inactive thyroid hormones into active ones. Her high blood pressure, lack of energy and loss of smell could be caused by this lack of nutrients. We discovered that Suzanne was not absorbing her nutrients, due to low hydrochloric acid in her stomach. This is a fairly common finding in elderly folks, where low hydrochloric acid can lead to low vitamin B12 levels and, subsequently, low energy and memory loss, along with high homocysteine levels, which is a high risk factor for cardiovascular disease and Osteoporosis.

I recommended a supplement program that included hydrochloric acid, liquid calcium and magnesium, and a liquid multivitamin and mineral blend to Suzanne to address these issues. We started with liquid nutrients as they are more readily absorbed. She returned in 30 days and reported that her blood pressure was down to 131/71 and her doctor had cut down on her thyroid medication. Her energy level had improved; her joints no longer hurt, but her hip was still stiff. Her colon was moving better overall, she still had some back pain and though her hair was still falling out, she was not losing the big clumps she used to. But she was most excited to report that she was able to taste food again – and this had happened exactly 30 hours after taking her first dose of supplements!

We continue to work with Suzanne at the clinic, and she is doing well. Her joint movement is much better, she has had no problems with her colon (no more hospital stays), she no longer gets the flu or colds like she used to, and her memory is continuing to improve. Best of all: She is able to play the piano again, which is the joy of her life! We expect a good report from her M.D. on the osteoporosis, as she is absorbing her minerals much better now, which leads to rebuilding bone. She has also been able to avoid hip surgery, because her hip strength is constantly improving.

REPEATED MISCARRIAGES

In the fall of 2001, I began to see Betty Jo, a stunning blonde with a brilliant zest for life. A keen and shrewd entrepreneur, Betty Jo had run two busy retail stores, but had sold them to become a stay-at-home mom. She and her supportive husband had a 3-year-old son, but they wanted to have more children. Several times, Betty Jo had tried to get pregnant, but, sadly, each time she was unable to sustain the pregnancy. She'd had three miscarriages since August 2000.

Each miscarriage devastated her and her husband. Naturally, the couple was getting very discouraged. Each miscarriage had occurred around the fifth or sixth week of the first trimester. Betty Jo also had painful but regular periods, and was experiencing brain fog, fatigue, and a craving for sweets. Blood sugar imbalances left her weak and shaky when she did not eat, and she also complained of gas and indigestion.

I tested her using the Wholistic Kinesiology method and determined that Betty Jo had a candida yeast infection problem. This can occur when antibiotics have been taken over a period of time; women can also get candida when taking birth control pills – and Betty Jo admitted that she had taken birth control bills for seven years prior to trying to get pregnant. Candida can lead to sweet cravings, blood sugar imbalances, brain fog, fatigue, and indigestion, as well as cause hormonal imbalances, which contribute to miscarriages.

I evaluated Betty Jo by using muscle testing techniques in an effort to see what would alleviate her problems, and found that she tested positive for some enzymes, candida support, blood sugar support and natural progesterone cream. In addition, I put her on the candida diet, which restricts sugars, yeasts, bread, some fruits, cheese, alcohol and fungus (mushrooms).

She returned 30 days later to report that her period was painless, her energy was much better, and her digestion had improved, especially when she stayed away from sugar. In addition, her thinking was much clearer.

I advised her to wait just a little before trying to get pregnant again and concentrate on getting as healthy as possible. By July 2002 she was feeling great and discovered that she was pregnant. We continued to monitor her and keep her on a supplement program to support pregnancy. She was on a prenatal vitamin, some natural progesterone, an antioxidant blend and some mild thyroid support. She was able to stay pregnant and carried her twin boys – *twins!!* – to full term with the help of Wholistic Kinesiology. Today, she and her husband have the three healthy and active children the couple always wanted!

Betty Jo was so impressed by her results that has gone on to become a Wholistic Kinesiology practitioner, and works on her family to keep them healthy using the techniques she learned. They are a very happy and healthy group! Betty Jo is in the process of opening her own clinic to begin practicing and helping others, and I wish her well.

NUTRASWEET ALLERGY

Jenny was a 32-year-old Hispanic woman with an easy smile, thick auburn hair and an inquisitive nature. She was an accountant and worked at a desk job, earning high marks from her supervisor during every employee evaluation. She was about to be married to a caring man. But she was also about to 100 pounds overweight, and had been struggling with her weight most of her life. Most of the foods and drinks she consumed contained aspartame, a synthetic sugar substitute that she thought was good because it allowed her to avoid sugar. On a routine visit to her physician, she was diagnosed with type II diabetes and given Metformin to control her blood sugar.

However, she had other complaints: neck and jaw pain, for which she wore a splint at night, low back pain, and hair loss. She couldn't lose weight and she had trouble controlling her blood sugar. She also had painful irregular periods.

Using muscle testing, I evaluated her and determined that her pancreas was extremely imbalanced. I further tested her to see which foods she should avoid, and found she was allergic to aspartame. I instructed her to avoid all artificial sweeteners and stay on a low-carb diet, then gave her a natural supplement to balance blood sugar levels and to balance hormone production in her pituitary gland. I also advised her to begin taking folic acid and a prenatal vitamin to help her get healthy towards eventually getting pregnant.

Jenny returned a month later and stated that her M.D. took her off her blood sugar medication as her blood sugar had completely normalized. Her neck and jaw pain has decreased significantly, and her energy was getting better by the day. She experienced no PMS, much less cramping in her period, which was now becoming regular as clockwork. During her follow-up visit a month later, she reported this happy news: She was pregnant! She had gotten pregnant on her wedding night!

Note: Aspartame is known as an excitotoxin – it actually kills neurons. According to Wikipedia, "The most well-known (to the general public) excitotoxic concern is the current debate over aspartame, also known as NutraSweet, and monosodium glutamate (MSG). Approximately 40% of aspartame (by mass) is broken down into the amino acid aspartic acid (also known as aspartate), an excitotoxin." In addition, it actually increases the desire for carbohydrates. Many people gain more weight on artificial sweeteners than if they weren't ingesting them.

DOG ALLERGY

Jason was a precocious 7-year-old boy who loved animals – especially dogs. He really enjoyed visiting family friends, particularly if there was a lively pooch in the house. Unfortunately, Jason was allergic to dog dander, which kept him from petting and playing with those canines. And he was extremely disappointed that his allergy prevented him from having a dog of his own. His mom brought him in to the clinic to see if there was anything we could do to help.

The muscle testing revealed that Jason was indeed allergic to dog dander. I decided to try a technique that has worked very well in this situation. Allergy Optimization, a non-invasive technique, which desensitizes the body to allergic substances, comes from the Nambudripod Allergy Elimination Technique developed by Dr. Devi Nambudripod.

Allergy Optimization instructs the body not to react to a certain substance in question. Good results are achieved by tapping the spine to stimulate the nervous system, tapping the thymus gland, and then tapping certain acupuncture points to stimulate the body to stay balanced when exposed to the substance in question. The client must hold the substance or have it near the body when desensitizing (The body sometimes develops these sensitivities inappropriately.)

We performed this painless technique in about 10 minutes. Several weeks later, I heard from Jason's mom that the family was able to get a new beagle puppy and that Jason had no allergic reactions to the dog. Snoopy has made Jason a very happy little boy!

HORMONAL CONFUSION

Dennis, a handsome and athletic 47-year-old man with curly black hair, was referred to me by Helen, his wife of 20 years. Dennis was a sensitive man, and a devoted husband and father, but he was in a lot of emotional pain and confusion. Helen had told me that she and Dennis were still married, but he had decided that he wanted to become a woman, and began the process of seeking sexual reassignment surgery, with the full intention of becoming a woman named Denise. As a prelude to the surgery, he had begun hormone therapy to complete the process of transformation.

About a month into this process, Dennis began to feel horrible and have regrets over his decision. The hormones made him feel irritable, fatigued, and extremely depressed. He suffered from insomnia. The medication also caused him to gain 40 pounds. Midway through the process, he changed his mind and decided to return to his life as a man and father. He stopped taking hormones and asked me to help him detox and get stable again.

Muscle testing revealed imbalances in Dennis's thyroid and adrenal glands, and excess estrogen and growth hormone in his blood system. I gave Dennis some herbal blends for balancing hormones and initiated emotional work using the Emotional Freedom Technique to help with his emotional pain and confusion.

Dennis returned a month later feeling really good. He had lost 14 pounds, his energy was returning and his sleep was improving. He was feeling much more emotionally stable and happy. Dennis has since decided to remain living his life as a man and is happily adjusting to his life.

CHRONIC FATIGUE AND SJOGREN'S SYNDROME

Gregorio's favorite hobby was rebuilding old horse carriages. He had been a carpenter in his native Greece, and brought that skill with him when he moved to America. Building cabinets paid the bills, but reconstructing in intricate detail, horse carriages used in the Wild West was his passion.

Unfortunately, the 52-year-old-man had not been able to use his tools or do much of anything for over a year. Gregorio was in a lot of misery; he experienced constant, terrible fatigue, headaches, Sjogren's Syndrome — severe dry eye syndrome — and constant joint pain. His health was getting steadily worse and worse, and physicians could not figure out why he was slowly descending into an incapacitated state. Blood tests and other lab work seemed to indicate that nothing was amiss. Finally, he was referred to me by a fellow chiropractor who was familiar with my Wholistic Kinesiology techniques.

I used the prioritization system to determine where Gregorio's problem was. The testing suggested he had a heavy metal toxicity problem, and I sent Gregorio for a six-hour urine test using a provocative substance called DMSA (dimercaptosuccinic acid). DMSA detects the presence of heavy metals in the body and can indicate relative levels of metals such as mercury, lead, arsenic, aluminum and other elements.

Gregorio's test returned 10 days later and revealed extremely high levels of lead and mercury. We collected the dust in the garage Gregorio had used to rebuild his carriages. The levels of lead were extremely high. We had our answer! According to the National Institute of Health, chronic lead exposure can cause:

- Irritability
- Aggressive behavior
- Low appetite and energy
- Difficulty sleeping
- Headaches
- Reduced sensations
- Loss of previous developmental skills (in young children)
- Anemia
- Constipation
- Abdominal pain and cramping (usually the first sign of a high, toxic dose of lead poison)
- Very high levels may cause vomiting, staggering gait, muscle weakness, seizures, or coma

We began Gregorio on a program of heavy metal chelation – the process of removing heavy metals from the body – using supplements he tested positive for. Chelating heavy metals is a slow process and requires monitoring on a consistent basis. We have to keep track of the routes of exit for the metals such as the liver, kidneys and colon. It took us many months to perform the chelation, but as the process continued, Gregorio began feeling so much better. His energy returned, his eye dryness greatly diminished, his thought processes cleared and his joint pain eased greatly.

Please note: There are some conditions that require some time to resolve. It can sometimes take *years* to undo some toxic situations that took a lifetime to accumulate. There are also some genetic defects that can impede the process. In addition, some people detoxify better then others. The beauty of the Wholistic Kinesiology technique is that it leads clients back to health as quickly and efficiently as possible without causing undo distress to the body. Many detox programs can leave one feeling out-of-sorts for long periods, as they are too harsh and intense for some people. In some cases, slow and steady is the best way to go.

CHRONIC EAR INFECTIONS

Jennifer was a 37-year-old African-American mother of three children. Her third child, Sylvia, was a precocious 8-month-old girl with dark black hair and striking dark eyes. She was also a very cranky kiddo, though, because she had been suffering with chronic ear infections since her birth. Her mother explained that her physician wanted to put tubes in the baby's ears to help with the drainage of mucus and, hopefully, prevent further infections. The baby's father, Bob, was horrified by that idea. He was familiar with Wholistic Kinesiology and pleaded with Jennifer to try this new approach.

Jennifer had a distressed look on her face when she brought Sylvia to see me. She was quite skeptical about alternative medicine, thinking it was nothing but woo-woo, feel-good affirmations and crystals. The only reason she was only trying this, she told me very matter-of-factly, was because of Bob's insistence.

I began by testing Sylvia for food allergies and other sensitivities. The first thing that became apparent was that she was extremely sensitive to dairy products. (According to Michael A Schmidt, M.D., dairy products are the most common culprit when it comes to ear infection and other childhood ear problems. Other things to watch for are wheat, eggs, chocolate, citrus, corn, soy, peanuts or other nuts, shellfish, sugar, and yeast.) Sylvia was being fed a dairy-based formula, as Jennifer was unable to breastfeed. Sylvia also had a yeast issue from all the antibiotics she had taken in her short life.

I recommended that Jennifer switch formulas to a non-dairy source, eliminate all dairy from the baby's diet, and give Sylvia acidophilus to replenish the beneficial bacteria in her intestines.

Jennifer was extremely reluctant to follow my instructions and her stony gaze expressed her reticence. Bob, however, was adamant that the other physicians had not helped the situation and urged Jennifer to give my instructions a try. Jennifer left shaking her head, but agreed to give it a go.

A week later, the couple returned for a follow-up visit. Jennifer reported that her baby's symptoms were completely gone and her physician cancelled the procedure to implant tubes. She was very surprised by the immediate turnaround in Sylvia, yet extraordinarily happy. She then made appointments for her other two children and herself. A few months later, she signed up for the six-month Wholistic Kinesiology course and became a practitioner herself!

Note: I love working with very young children because it can have a very profound effect on that child's future. These kinds of scenarios often lead to prescribed medications such as Antibiotics, subsequent yeast problems, food sensitivities and behavior and attention problems later. It is so rewarding to know you have prevented a rash of problems in the future.

PART III

WHOLISTIC KINESIOLOGY:

TECHNIQUES AND EXERCISES

CHAPTER 5
GETTING STARTED: IMPORTANT TERMS

Now that you have a good grasp of the theory of Wholistic Kinesiology, and you have read some actual case studies that demonstrate how Wholistic Kinesiology is used, it is time to try Wholistic Kinesiology yourself with a willing volunteer. This book is meant to guide you through the process in a safe, easy manner.

But first a few caveats. As I stated earlier, the information contained in this instruction manual is not intended to replace the services of a professional, licensed healthcare practitioner. The ultimate responsibility for treatment rests with you. If you or the person you are working with have a serious medical condition, please consult a licensed physician or therapist. Working toward healing yourself and others is our goal, but please realize that you may need the help of a trained professional if you are dealing with a serious condition.

My goal in writing this book was to provide new, intriguing information to people at all levels of medical competence. I hope that *all* people have a passion for seeking wellness. So, whether you have very little knowledge of medicine and medical terminology, or a deep background in healthcare – either traditional or alternative – you will be able to understand the principles and workings of Wholistic Kinesiology.

If you belong to the first group – readers who are unfamiliar with medical terminology – please do not feel like you need to suddenly cram eight years of medical school into your head. You do not have to memorize all the following terms and body points to understand Wholistic Kinesiology. But you may want to bookmark these sections so you can refer back to them easily. And to my physician and nursing friends: These terms may seem like second nature to you, but I believe you will also learn something new here!

ANATOMICAL TERMS

Here is a list of common terms used to describe how to locate monitor points on the body. (To review the section on monitor points, see Chapter 3: "Principles of Applied Kinesiology" and Chapter 6: "Muscle Testing and Monitor Points.")

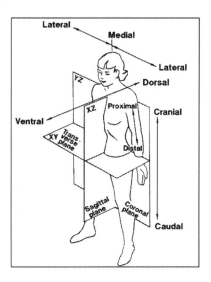

Anatomical position: Standing erect, with palms facing forward.

Anterior/Ventral: Situated at or directed toward the front side of the body.

Bilateral: The points are situated on either sides of the vertical midline (an imaginary line that runs from chin to pubic bone). These points are only on one side, unless the point description states "bilateral simultaneously".

Caudad: Located away from the head.

Cephalad/Cranial: Located toward the head.

Distal: Located further away from the center of a specific area. Think "distant."

Fontanel: Either of the two meetings of three suture lines of the skull, otherwise known as "soft spots."

Finger: A measure of distance. On the torso, it is the width of a fingertip; on the face or head, it is the depth of a fingertip.

Inch (body inch): Unit of measurement; the distance from the first to the second joint of a tightly bent index finger. On the face/head, we use a 1/2-body-inch as a standard unit of measure.

Inferior: Below.

Insertion: The end of a muscle, which is attached to the freely moving bone of its joint. It is at the opposite end of the muscle "origin."

Lateral: Away from the midline.

Medial: Toward the vertical midline.

Midline: The imaginary line that divides the body into right and left sides.

Origin: The end of a muscle that is attached to the relatively fixed bone of its joint. It is at the opposite end of the muscle "insertion."

Posterior/Dorsal: The back side of anatomical position, includes soles of feet.

Superior: Above.

BODY LANDMARKS

The following landmarks are also important to know, and will help you find the monitor and evaluation points on the body. If you would like to familiarize yourself better with these landmarks, feel free to highlight the points by placing the numbers on the skeleton diagrams on the next pages.

I. **ASIS** – Anterior Superior Iliac Spine: the prominent bony protrusions of the hips on the front of the body (bilateral)

2. **Angle of Louis** – Sternum at the level of second rib, where two bones of sternum meet. Usually a small bump is prominent.

3. **Anterior Fontanel** – The slight indentation on the crest of the midline of the head. The front "soft spot."

4. **Atlas** – The first cervical vertebra in the neck,(feel the sides of it just under the skull below your ears).

5. **Axis** – The second cervical vertebra.

6. **Cervical Vertebra** – The seven spinal segments in the neck; also referred to as CI-C7.

7. **Chin** – The tip of the bone, not the flesh.

8. **Clavicle** – Collar bone.

9. **Coracoid Process** – Junction of the scapula, humerus (upper arm bone) and clavicle.

10. **Coronal Suture** – Suture where the frontal and parietal bones of the skull meet.

II. **Episternal Notch** – Indentation at top of sternum.

12. **Frontal Eminence** – Bony projections between the eyebrows and hairline.

13. **Glabella Protrusion** – Brow ridge; the bony ridge just over the eyes.

14. **Hairline** – The original hairline if the hair has receded.

15. **Intercostal Space** – Space between any two ribs.

16. **Lambdoidal Suture** – Suture between parietal (side cranial) and occipital bones (one in back).

17. **Lumbar Vertebra** – The five lowest vertebra in the back; also referred to as LI-L5.

18. **Mandible** – The lower jaw.

19. **Masseter** – The large jaw muscle felt by gritting teeth.

20. **Nipple Line** – The vertical midline of half the frontal view of chest. (Note: This is different from the nipple level).

21. **Nose, Midpoint** – Midpoint between tip of nose and glabella protrusion.

22. **Occipital Protuberance** – Protrusions a few inches lateral to midline at rear base of skull (bilateral).

23. **Posterior Fontanel** – Junction of occipital and parietal bones on top of the head; posterior soft spot.

24. **Pubic Bone** – The midline bony point just above the genitals.

25. **Ramus of Mandible** – Corners of the lower jaw.

26. **SCM** –Sterno-cleido-mastoid muscle; prominent muscle on side of neck.

27. **Scapula** – Shoulder blades in back.

28. **Thenar Eminence** – Pad at the base of the thumb bilateral.

29. **Thoracic Vertebra** – The twelve vertebra in the middle of the spine; also referred to as TI-TI2.

30. **Thyroid Cartilage** – The shield-shaped cartilage of the upper and lower neck.

31. **Xyphoid Process** – Small projection at end of the sternum.

32. **Zygomatic Process** – Lower part of the bone forming the hard part of the cheek.

Use the diagrams to locate these points and place the corresponding numbers on the skeletons. This is a good way to learn the location of these landmarks.

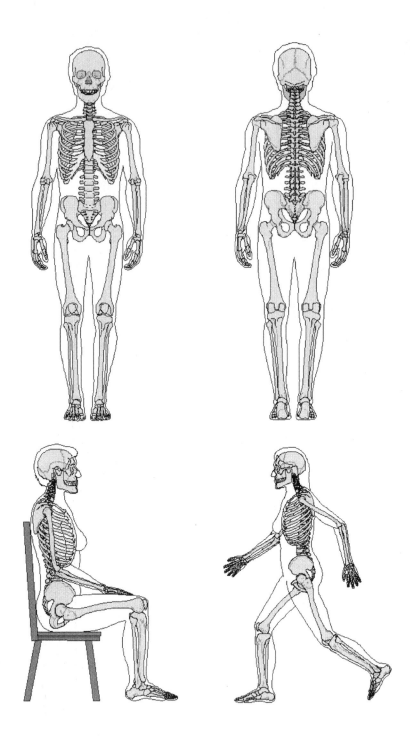

ORGAN SWEEP

Think of the organ sweep directory as a list of important points on the body you can use to test the wellness of organs, hormones or other circumstances that affect the health of one's organs. This list is by no means comprehensive, but checking the areas specified below will yield a lot of good information about corresponding organs and what may be affecting them. As you become more adept at practicing Wholistic Kinesiology, you may add other areas of concern to this list.

The order of these points is designed to be tested on the body from the bottom up starting at the pubic bone to make it easier to memorize. (Refer to the previous "Anatomical Terms" and "Body Landmarks" lists for definitions):

1. **Prostate/Vagina**-Midline on the public bone.
2. **Heavy Metal Toxicity**-Midline pubic bone, two fingers superior.
3. **Bladder:** Midline, pubic bone, 1 inch superior.
4. **Ovaries:** Bilateral, 1 inch medial to ASIS.
5. **Estrogen Imbalance:** Right ovary and uterus points simultaneously.
6. **Progesterone Imbalance:** Midpoint between ASIS and uterus point, left side.
7. **Uterus:** Midline, at level of ASIS.
8. **Cardiovascular Health:** Bilateral, 1 inch lateral to navel, 1 inch inferior.
9. **Ileocecal Valve:** Right side navel, ASIS midpoint.
10. **Ileum:** Right side navel, ASIS midpoint 1 finger superior.
11. **Kidney:** Bilateral, 1 inch lateral to midline at level of navel (also test over the organ on the posterior side just under the ribcage).
12. **Pancreas:** Midline navel, 1 inch superior.
13. **Colon:** Apply lateral edge of hand over each section (ascending, transverse, descending, and sigmoid).
14. **Gallbladder:** Right side, 10th rib tip.
15. **Stomach:** Bilateral and midline, navel and tip of xyphoid process, 2 fingers inferior to midpoint and 1 inch lateral simultaneously.
16. **Liver:** Right side, costal cartilage, 8-9 intercostal space (or just place hand over liver area on right ribcage).
17. **Spleen:** Left side, costal cartilage, 8-9 intercostal space.

18. **Parasite:** Bilateral, ASIS one inch superior.

19. **Adrenal medulla:** Bilateral, tip of xyphoid process, 1 1/2 inches inferior and over to ribcage edge.

20. **Adrenal cortex:** Bilateral, thenar eminence, midpoint (pad at base of thumb).

21. **Candida:** Bilateral, 1 finger lateral to tip of xyphoid process, 2 fingers inferior.

22. **HCL Level:** Left side, xyphoid process edge.

23. **Implanted Virus:** (these are chronic virus' such as Herpes, Epstein-Barr, Hepatitis C, etc.) Two inches inferior to xyphoid process.

24. **Lung:** Bilateral, 1/2 inch lateral to midline at nipple level, 1 inch superior.

25. **Allergy:** Midline, tip of xyphoid process and episternal notch, 1 finger superior to point, ¼ distance cephalad.

26. **Digestion:** Midline, at sternum, 2 fingers superior to midpoint.

27. **Heart:** Left side, at sternum, 3-4 intercostal space.

28. **Lymph:** Bilateral, 1/2 inch lateral to midline, Angle of Louis (the junction of the manubrium and sternum on the midline).

29. **Thymus:** Midline, Angle of Louis.

30. **Thyroid:** Bilateral, 1/2 inch lateral to midline episternal notch, 1 inch superior.

31. **Fungus:** Bilateral, SCM midpoint.

32. **Bacteria:** Midline, lower lip, 2 fingers inferior to lower border.

33. **General Nutrition:** Bilateral, touching cheek with tongue, point to side of cheek.

34. **Sinus:** Bilateral on pupil line, orbit, inferior and superior aspects.

35. **Pituitary:** Midline, glabella protrusion.

36. **High Blood Sugar:** Left side, ½ inch medial to pupil line, eyebrow and frontal eminence, ¾ distance cephalad.

37. **Low Blood Sugar:** Right side, ½ inch medial to pupil line, eyebrow and frontal eminence, ¾ distance cephalad.

38. **Virus:** (This is a more acute virus such as a cold) Midline, four fingers superior to frontal eminence.

39. **Arterial Health:** Four fingers along space between thyroid cartilage and SCM muscle bilateral.

The Organ Sweep list is an abridged version of the more comprehensive "Wholistic Kinesiology Monitor Points list that you will find in the next chapter. The Organ Sweep list contains the most important areas of the body — areas that I believe every kinesiology practitioner should pay attention to, so one does not accidentally overlook something important.

CHAPTER 6
MUSCLE TESTING AND MONITOR POINTS

Put simply, a muscle test is a brief but firm pull against a part of the body in a direction that isolates a muscle or group of muscles for the purpose of monitoring that muscle's ability to function. The object is not to gauge the muscle's absolute strength but, rather, to see how quickly and firmly the muscle responds to the test.

There are two types of muscles tests:

    * *Structural muscle test* — A test that gives information about that muscle's own strength and condition.

    * *Indicator test* — Used as a primary feedback tool, this test gives information about other parts of the body.

Keep this in mind: Muscle responses change instantly in reaction to environmental factors and other variables that may be purposefully or inadvertently introduced during testing. The power of the indicator test is that it can provide reliable "yes/no" responses, thereby allowing the body to speak for itself. The response will be identical when using any muscle in the body.

For purposes of convenience, we most commonly use a muscle group in the shoulder for testing our client. This muscle group is composed of the anterior deltoid, trapezius, and pectoralis muscles. Whichever muscle or muscle group is chosen will be called the **indicator muscle**. That muscle must test strong in the clear (before any stimulus is applied) for it to be considered useful as an indicator muscle.

The person being tested may sit, stand or lie down. However, I have found that it is most convenient and easier for the person if he or she is lying down (see Figure 1). Avoid music, flashing lights, strong smells, or loud noises during the testing session. Sudden or surprising events can cause the client to "switch out" (lose concentration and switch the nervous system responses off), making the testing unreliable. Minimize extraneous variables as much as possible during the session.

Procedure:

1. Have the client lie down, and keep the individual's eyes open and looking straight ahead. Wearing glasses, a watch, or jewelry will not adversely effect the testing session. You want to test the client as he or she normally functions in the world. If the client is particularly sensitive, you can remove all jewelry to increase accuracy.

2. Make sure the client's hands are not touching his or her body, and the feet are not crossed.

3. Make sure that the muscle you will be using for the testing session is not injured or sore.

4. Ask the client to raise his or her arm into the air with the elbow locked, while making a loose fist. The tester should place a hand on the back of the client's wrist with the client's elbow slightly bent. Either arm can be used, but make sure that the muscle is strong before adding any variable to the testing.

5. Slowly and gently apply pressure to the back of the client's wrist and lifting in an upward direction, (using a pulling motion up on the wrist) while asking the client to resist the pressure. Do it for a few seconds, then gradually increase the pressure. You are looking for a "lock in" of the muscle. You should feel the client's shoulder rise off the table slightly as it locks in. **NOTE:** Do not maintain the pressure for too long, and do not surprise the client by pushing too suddenly and without warning. As you gain experience, you will be able to apply less force to feel "strong" and "weak" reactions.

6. After establishing what a "strong" test feels like for this client, introduce variables into the equation, to feel what a "weak" test will feel like. For example, put a substance next to the person that would be considered poisonous, such as chlorine bleach. Retest the muscle; it should test weak or mushy compared to the previous muscle test.

Remember, this is not a contest of strength! You want to measure the client's nervous system's ability to respond to a command. When the nervous system is functioning properly, the muscle will lock in and test "strong." When there is an interference of some sort, it will not lock in and will test "weak." Do not let these terms confuse you into thinking this is a test of strength. This is a nervous system response, not a muscle response. (Actually, this technique should probably be called "nervous system testing" instead of muscle testing.)

Different people will feel differently when being tested. Testing as many people as possible in the beginning of one's practice will be very helpful. Remember: This technique may take awhile to perfect. So try not to get frustrated in the beginning. Just keep at it!

Tip: This is the most important part of the entire process. Take your time to really "feel" the "lock in" of the arm and the "unlock" that you get with a weak response. This is critical to your success. If you are unsure about the response, test it again and give a little more pressure with an upward pulling motion. Staying neutral about your expected answers is also paramount to accuracy. If you have already made up your mind that the response should go a certain way, this may cause you to get inaccurate answers. Listen with an open mind to what the body is trying to say!

Figure I: Muscle Testing

THERAPY LOCALIZATION

Kinesiological research has located points on the surface of the body that are connected to organs or organ functions. These points are stimulated when touched; when this happens, a connection is made. In other words, a muscle test performed while touching the point, creates a useful way to check the functioning of the organ, gland or body system wired via the nervous system to that point.

If the test muscle is strong, the body part or function is balanced and all is well with the particular organ, gland or body system. But if the test muscle is weak, some measure of imbalance is present. We call touching these points *therapy localization.* Many of these points have their origin in acupuncture; some were developed through trial and error, while others lie directly over the organ in question.

When touching the point, make sure that your fingertip is perpendicular to the skin and that you do not slide your finger across the skin to find the point you want to test. Unless otherwise stated, the index finger should be used to touch the points.

Monitor Points and Evaluation Points

There are two kinds of points: monitor points and evaluation points. A **monitor point** represents a body system, function or nutritional level, and will test strong to the extent that this area of the body is healthy.

An **evaluation point** draws on the body's innate wisdom to know which type of nutrient or therapy it needs to attain a state of wellness. To be useful, the test muscle *must* be "strong in the clear" before introducing a sample of a substance (vitamin, supplement, suggestion of a therapy, etc.) to the client, because the muscle may or may not become weak when exposed to the sample.

Here are some easy sample tests you can try.

Steps for using a **monitor** point:
1. Find a strong test muscle (indicator muscle).
2. Use the testing readiness procedure. (See Chapter 7: "Using Wholistic Kinesiology")

3. Test for polarity. (See Chapter 7)
4. Touch a monitor point from the list of points and then retest the test muscle.

If the test muscle remains strong, the point is balanced. If it goes weak, an imbalance is present.

Steps for using an **evaluation** point:
1. Find a strong test muscle.
2. Use the testing readiness procedure (introduced in the next chapter).
3. Test for Polarity (introduced in the next chapter).
4. Touch an evaluation point on your body with a fingertip (such as the health remedy point introduced further in the book), and then retest the test muscle to establish that the evaluation point is strong. While still touching the point, introduce the body to the substance or therapy and retest the muscle.

If the test muscle remains strong, the substance or therapy currently meets the evaluation point's criteria for usefulness for your system. If the test muscle goes weak, the substance does not meet those criteria for your system at this time. We use these points to test for beneficial nutrients or adverse reactions such as an allergic response to a food, etc.

Keep in mind:
- Placing the substance within one inch of the body is going to give the best response in general.
- It is important to locate the points as accurately as possible to insure that you are testing the specific organ or body system you want, and not some other organ or body system.

WHOLISTIC KINESIOLOGY MONITOR POINTS

This is a more comprehensive list of monitor points than the "Organ Sweep" list presented in Chapter 5. This list presents the item to be tested for in bold letters, and where the corresponding monitor point can be found on the body. If need be, consult the "Anatomical Terms" and "Body Landmarks" lists in Chapter 5.

If you are coming to this for the first time, please do not feel you need to muscle test every single item on this list — doing so might take you hours! Instead practice with a few of these monitor points, and as you gain confidence with this technique, add more points to your repertoire.

Absorption/assimilation, midline, sternum at midpoint.

Acidophilus level: right, at costal cartilage and tip of xyphoid process, 4-finger contact just inferior under the ribcage.

Adenoids: midline nose, tip of cartilage.

Adrenal cortex: bilateral, thenar eminence, midpoint.

Adrenal medulla: bilateral, at costal cartilage tip of xyphoid process, 1 1/2 inches inferior.

Adrenal hormones: midline tip of xyphoid process, 2 inches inferior.

Allergies: midline, tip of xyphoid process and episternal notch, 1-finger superior to point, 1/4 distance cephalad.

Allergy (tissue or skin reaction): bilateral, 1 inch lateral to midline chin, 1 inch superior to tip.

Aorta: right at sternum, 4-5 intercostal space.

Androgens: midpoint, between tip of chin, episternal notch, 1 1/2 inches lateral left side.

Appendix: right side midpoint between ASIS and navel 1 inch inferior.

Arterial plaque: midline, tip of xyphoid process and episternal notch, 1 finger superior to point, 1/4 distance cephalad.

Bacteria: midline, lower lip, 2 fingers inferior to lower border.

Bladder: midline, pubic bone, 1 inch superior.

Blood (general): midline, tip of xyphoid process and episternal notch, I-finger inferior to point, 3/4 distance cephalad.

Blood allergy: midline, lower and upper thyroid cartilage's midpoint.

Blood pH: midline, episternal notch, I-inch inferior.

Blood pressure (high): left, 3 ½ inches lateral to midline clavicle, superior aspect.

Blood pressure (low): right, 3 ½ inches lateral to midline clavicle, superior aspect.

Blood toxicity: midline, nose I-inch superior to midpoint.

Bone (general): bilateral, I-inch lateral to sternum, 5-6 intercostal space.

Bone tissue: bilateral on nipple line, 7-8 intercostal space.

Brain (general): bilateral, I-inch lateral to midline frontal eminence, I inch superior.

Bronchioles: midline, sternum, apply medial aspect of hand with fingers straightly extended to body of sternum.

Candida: bilateral, I finger lateral to midline tip of xyphoid process, 2 fingers inferior.

Capillaries: midline tip of typhoid process, 2 fingers inferior.

Cerebellum: midline bony protuberance at back of skull, I-finger superior.

Cerebrum: bilateral, ¼ inch lateral to midline, anterior and posterior fontanels midpoint.

Cerebrospinal fluid: midline, anterior fontanel, 5 fingers posterior.

Cervix: midline, pubic bone, 2 fingers superior.

Circulation in extremities: bilateral on nipple line, navel, I-finger superior.

Colon: midline or bilateral, colon, apply small finger edge of hand over sections.

Coronary arteries: right at Sternum, 1-2 intercostal space.

Cranial nerves: midline, nose 1 inch superior to tip of cartilage.

Depression: midline, anterior fontanel.

Digestion (general): midline, sternum, 2 fingers superior to midpoint.

Duodenum: navel and tip of xyphoid process, 1 inch inferior to midpoint, 5 fingers lateral on the right side only.

Ears (outer & canal): bilateral, ear canal.

Ear (inner): bilateral, ear canal opening, 1-inch anterior.

Ear (middle): bilateral, ear canal opening, 1-finger anterior.

Energy: nipple line, navel intersection, right side.

Enzymes: midline, lower lip, inferior border.

Estrogen: bilateral, midline and 1 inch medial, ASIS simultaneously, right side.

Fallopian tubes: bilateral, 2 inches lateral to midline, ASIS 2 fingers superior.

Free radical toxicity: midline, ASIS, 1-inch inferior.

Fungus: bilateral, SCM muscle midpoint.

Gallbladder: right, 10th rib tip.

Heart: left at sternum, 3-4 intercostal space.

Heavy metals: midline, pubic bone, 2 fingers superior.

Hemorrhoids: bilateral, one inch lateral to midline, on line between midline and ASIS, 2 fingers inferior.

Hypothalamus: bilateral on superior temporal line, glabella protrusion and hairline midpoint.

Ileocecal valve: right navel and ASIS midpoint.

Ileum: right navel and ASIS, I finger superior to midpoint.

Immune system: bilateral on nipple line, 5-6 intercostal space.

Immunoreactive response (autoimmune): midline, anterior fontanel, 2 fingers posterior.

Implanted Virus: 2 inches inferior to xyphoid process.

Infection (general): midline, tip of xyphoid process, 2 inches inferior.

Insulin: bilateral, I inch lateral to midline navel, 4 fingers superior.

Jejunum: right, 5 fingers lateral to midline, navel and tip of xyphoid process, 4 fingers inferior to midpoint.

Joint: bilateral, at sternum, 2-3 intercostal space.

Kidney: bilateral, I-inch lateral to midline.

Kidney stones: midline, navel, 4 fingers inferior.

Large intestine toxicity: midline navel and tip of xyphoid process, 4 fingers superior to midpoint.

Libido: nipple line and navel intersection, left side.

Liver (general): right on nipple line, navel and tip of xyphoid process, I-inch inferior to midpoint.

Lung: bilateral, I/2-inch lateral to midline nipple, I-inch superior.

Lymph: bilateral, I/2-inch lateral to midline, angle of Louis.

Malignancy: bilateral, 1 1/2 inches lateral to midline, 3-4 intercostal space.

Meridians: midline, chin, 1-finger superior to tip.

Migraine: midline, bridge of nose.

Minerals (general): midline, episternal notch, 1-finger inferior.

Muscles (general): bilateral, 2 fingers lateral to midline navel and tip of xyphoid process, 1-finger superior to midpoint.

Muscle tissue: midline, tip of xyphoid, 2 inches inferior.

Nephro(kidney)/Urinary (general): bilateral, 1-inch lateral to midline, navel and tip of xyphoid process, 2 fingers superior to midpoint.

Nerve impulse: bilateral on nipple line, 2-3 intercostal space.

Nerve tissue: bilateral at sternum, 2-3 intercostal space.

Nervous system-parasympathetic: bilateral at sternum, 5-6 intercostal space.

Nervous system-sympathetic: bilateral on nipple line, 4-5 intercostal space.

Nutrition (general): bilateral, touching cheek tongue point, tongue toward side of mouth at space between teeth.

Ovaries: bilateral, 1-inch medial to ASIS.

Pancreas: midline, navel, 1-inch superior.

Pancreatic enzymes: midline, navel, 5 fingers superior.

Parasites: Bilateral, ASIS 1 inch superior

Parathyroid: bilateral, 1-inch lateral to midline episternal notch, 1-inch superior.

Parasitic candida: midline, quadriceps muscle, midpoint.

Pineal: midline, glabella protrusion, 2 fingers superior.

Pituitary: midline, glabella protrusion.

Pituitary hormones: left and right ½ inch lateral to midline glabella protrusion.

Platelets: midline, episternal notch, 2 fingers inferior.

Portal vein: midline, tip of xyphoid process, 5 fingers inferior.

Precancerous chromosome changes: midline, navel and tip of xyphoid process, 2 fingers inferior to midpoint.

Progesterone: midpoint between ASIS and navel at the level of the ASIS, left side.

Prostate: midline, pubic bone.

Radiation toxicity: midline, episternal notch, 4 fingers inferior.

Red blood cells: midline, on sternum, 2 fingers superior to point, 3/4 distance cephalad.

Serotonin level: bilateral, I-inch lateral to midline anterior and posterior fontanels, I-finger posterior to midpoint.

Sinus (frontal): bilateral, on pupil line, ocular orbit, superior aspect.

Sinus (maxillary): bilateral, on pupil line, inferior aspect.

Skin: midline, frontal eminence.

Sleep: atop xyphoid process tip.

Small intestine: place hand over abdomen below navel.

Spinal cord: midline, anterior fontanel, I-finger posterior.

Spleen: left at costal cartilage, 8-9 intercostal space.

Stomach: bilateral and midline, navel and tip of xyphoid process, 2 fingers inferior to midpoint and I inch lateral simultaneously.

Temperature regulation: midline, tip of xyphoid process and episternal notch, 2 fingers inferior to point, ¼ distance cephalad.

Tendons: midline, frontal eminence, I-finger inferior.

Testosterone: pubic bone, I 1/2 inches lateral left side.

Thalamus: bilateral, on superior temporal line, glabella protrusion and hairline, 2 fingers superior to midpoint.

Thyroid: bilateral, I/2 inch lateral to midline episternal notch, I-inch superior.

Thymus: midline, angle of Louis.

Tonsils: midline, chin, 2 fingers inferior to tip.

Toxicity (deep tissue): midline, ASIS, I-inch inferior.

Ureter: midline, pubic bone, I-finger superior.

Uterus: midline, ASIS.

Vertebrae: midline, tip of xyphoid process, 2 fingers superior to point I/4 distance caudad from episternal notch.

Vitamins: bilateral at sternum, 5-6 intercostal space. (For a list of vitamins, minerals, nutrients and amino acids, see Chapter 8: "Evaluating Levels of Imbalance.)

Virus (general): midline, frontal eminence, 4 fingers superior

Virus (implanted): midline, xyphoid process two inches inferior.

Vision: bilateral, I/2 inch lateral to pupil line, frontal eminence and hairline midpoint.

Water retention: midline, pubic bone 4 fingers superior.

Weight: midline, glabella protrusion, 2 fingers inferior.

White blood cells: midline, tip of xyphoid process and episternal notch, I-finger superior to point, 3/4 distance cephalad.

Yeast: midline, chin, I-inch inferior to tip.

Nutrition Points

1. **General nutrition** – Bilateral, point tongue to side of mouth and touch outside of cheek.

2. **General mineral** – Midline, episternal notch, 1 finger inferior.

3. **General vitamin** – Bilateral at sternum, 5-6 intercostal space.

4. **Bioflavonoid** – Left 1/2 inch lateral to midline clavicle, inferior aspect.

5. **Dietary fats** – Bilateral 4th toe, ventral surface, distal phalanx.

6. **Intestinal B vitamins** – Bilateral, ASIS, midpoint from midline.

7. **Protein** – Midline, thyroid cartilage, upper.

8. **Calcium** – Left claviculosternal junction, superior aspect.

9. **Chromium** – Midline, ASIS, 1/2 inch inferior.

10. **Copper** – Left navel and ASIS, 1 inch inferior to midpoint.

11. **Iron** – Midpoint on right inguinal ligament (ligament runs between pubic bone and ASIS).

12. **Magnesium** – Midline, navel.

13. **Manganese** – Midline, ASIS, 1 inch inferior.

14. **Phosphorus** – Right, at sternum, 2-3 intercostal space.

15. **Potassium** – Right, masseter muscle surface.

16. **Selenium** – Midline, navel 4 fingers inferior.

17. **Silica** – Left at costal cartilage, 7-8 intercostal space.

18. **Sodium** – Left, masseter muscle surface.

19. **Sulfur** – Left at sternum, 2-3 intercostal space.

20. **Trace minerals** – Bilateral, sternocleido mastoid muscle, immediately posterior to midpoint.

21. **Vitamin A** – Right eyeball.

22. **Vitamin B complex** – Midline tongue.

23. **Vitamin C** – Left 1 1/2 inches lateral to midline clavicle inferior aspect.

24. **Vitamin D** – Left inguinal ligament, midpoint.

25. **Vitamin E (fat soluble)** – Right, 1 1/2 inches lateral to midline.

26. **Vitamin E complex** – Left, directly inferior to axilla, 7-8 intercostal space.

27. **Vitamin F** – Right, claviculosternal junction, superior aspect.

28. **Vitamin K** – Midline, thyroid cartilage, 2 fingers inferior to lower.

29. **Zinc** – Right, navel and ASIS, 1 inch inferior to midpoint.

CHAPTER 7
THE WHOLISTIC KINESIOLOGY
TESTING PROCESS

This flow chart is the standard "road map" of what a Wholistic Kinesiology session looks like. On this page, you will find the order of muscle tests that are performed. Each step will be further discussed in this chapter.

On the next page, you will find the methodology map of muscle testing to evaluate the imbalance in the body. Following those steps will help you determine the right type of therapy, vitamin(s) or supplement(s) your client's body needs to correct the imbalance. (For a more detailed discussion of these steps, see Chapter 8: "Testing for Nutritional Needs.")

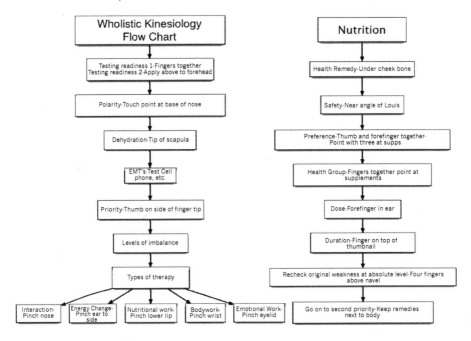

TESTING READINESS PROCESS

Wholistic Kinesiology uses the **"Testing Readiness"** process to determine a body's ability to give accurate information about its needs through muscle testing. It also indicates that the client's body is willing to trust you. This trust creates a circuit of information between you and your client. A strong test indicates both the client's willingness to trust you and your client's body's ability to draw on its innate wisdom to communicate its needs during a testing session.

Just watch out for "switching out," where certain imbalances confuse muscle response and convert muscle-testing results into random or reversed answers, which then negates their usefulness as an analytic tool. In other words, getting a strong test does not indicate whether or not, in the long term, you might be fooled by an occasional "switching out" response. Therefore, you must realize that it is possible to get reliable answers at the moment, even if deeper imbalances are present.

Keep this rule in mind:

The testing readiness process must remain strong throughout every testing session.

For example, hearing a sudden loud noise, getting up and walking around, becoming dehydrated, or needing to go to the bathroom are some of the many factors that can cause imbalances in the client, which may alter the client's ability to give correct answers. If test results become unclear or inconsistent during a session, go back to the Testing Readiness process and reorient the client as needed.

Normally, a strong Testing Readiness test on the client means that the circuit between you and your client will be consistent. But remember: Either yours or your client's neurological or energy imbalances can disturb the accuracy of a session. You may want to check both of you before beginning the session. When you are first learning to muscle test, "switching out" can be very common. But as you gain experience, you will find that it happens much less often.

Testing Readiness Procedure:
1. Find a strong indicator muscle.
2. **Testing Readiness One**: Have the client put all fingers and thumb together in a bunch. (See Figure 2.) Test the indicator muscle.

3. If the test muscle becomes weak while holding this hand pose, use any of the following therapies to strengthen it:

    a. Drink water.

    b. With either a circular or back and forth motion, lightly rub the area between the navel and the ribcage on the midline for about thirty seconds.

    c. Do crosscrawl patterns.

    d. Use some Bach Flower rescue remedy under the tongue

4. Repeat step two.

5. When holding this hand pose no longer weakens the client's indicator muscle, move to testing to system check two.

6. **Testing Readiness Two:** Have the client apply bunched fingers to the forehead between the glabella protrusion and the frontal eminence. (See Figure 2.) Recheck indicator muscle. If weak, apply pressure to the atlas transverse process (under the skull and below the ear) and rub vigorously on the right or left side. (Rub on the side that tests strong while the client is holding the hand pose.)

7. Recheck by testing bunched fingers on forehead.

8. When strong, your system is ready to let body wisdom speak clearly.

Testing Readiness usually stays in effect for a testing session, but if testing becomes unclear or inconsistent, check it again and repeat therapies.

Figure 2: System Check One

Figure 3: System Check Two

Neurological Switching:
Cross Crawl Remedy

If the client tends to "switch out" frequently (test weak on the Testing Readiness Process), doing some form of a cross crawl pattern might be helpful. This exercise is helpful, because it activates areas in both brain hemispheres at the same time. The result is better, faster and more integrated communication between the two hemispheres, which creates a higher level of reasoning and openness – which is needed for reliable muscle testing results.

The following description of cross crawl is just one variation of this procedure. If the version presented below does not produce a strong response, there are other variations of cross crawl you can test for. In fact, hundreds of variations are possible: Any movement that involves diagonally opposite arms and legs can be combined with any motion of the head or eyes, and you can even add humming, counting, singing or talking.

Procedure:

1. Lie on your back with your legs straight and your arms at your sides.
2. Inhale and bring your left arm to your right knee as you bend it and lift toward your chest. (See Figure 4.)
3. Lower the arm and leg to a neutral position while exhaling.
4. Repeat the full cycle with the other arm and leg (Figure 5), inhaling up and exhaling down.
5. Generally, ten repetitions will help reset the body for the testing session. This exercise may be done daily for those who tend to switch out frequently, or who have some form of learning disorder.

Figure 4: Cross Crawl 1

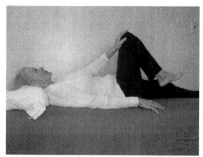

Figure 5: Cross Crawl 2

Polarity

Checking the polarity – the alignment of opposing tendencies within the body of the person being tested (Figure 6) – will also give you information that the client is testable and is giving you accurate answers. The client may test strong on the Testing Readiness Process but may really be in "overdrive" – a state of extreme stress and adrenal hyperfunction, where all evaluations test strong and the results are unreliable. Therefore, getting a weak response on the polarity test will give you an idea of how the client will respond "weakly," and will assure that you will be able to recognize what a weak response will look like in the future.

This test is performed by touching the area just below the glabella protrusion, where the nose joins the face.

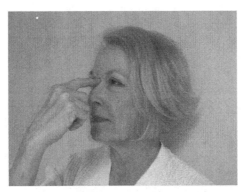

Figure 6: Polarity test

It should test *weak* in the clear if the person is testable. If the test is strong, generally it means that the person is in "overdrive," and you may get inaccurate answers in your testing. Using some procedure or substance to ground the client may be necessary, like:

Deep relaxing breathing or meditation
Bach Flower Rescue Remedy (spray or drops)
Digestive enzymes
Adrenal Glandular Support (a stress-buster)
Supplemental RNA/DNA substance

Coenzymate B Vitamins (boosts mental abilities)
DSF Formula (By Nutriwest)

All of the products mentioned above can be found in most health food or vitamin supplement stores. Have the person ingest the substance(s) and then retest the polarity point. Do not proceed until this point tests "weak," as your results will be unreliable.

TESTING FOR DEHYDRATION

Water is essential for nutrient assimilation, waste removal and for proper functioning of the nervous system. Therefore, it is very important to test hydration and water quality on your clients.

In general, most people do not drink enough water. The general rule is to drink half one's weight in ounces. For example, someone who weighs 150 pounds should consume 75 ounces of water per day. The body, however, can only assimilate 5 ounces at a time. So, drink small amounts throughout the day – not just one huge gulp a day to get it over with. People are often surprised to learn how much they have suppressed their thirst. It is often confused with other sensations such as hunger, confusion, annoyance, headaches, tiredness or inability to cope. Even small degrees of dehydration can interfere with nerve transmission and deplete the subtle energy of the body.

The municipal water supplies in general are not the best choice in drinking water. Spring or distilled water with electrolytes added is a better choice. But you can test for the most beneficial type of water to consume.

To test for **dehydration:**

Touch the lower tip of the either scapula (Figure 7). A weak test indicates the need for more water.

Figure 7: Test for Dehydration

To test for **water quality:**

1. Gently tug top of ear diagonally toward top and back of head (Figure 8). Test a previously strong muscle.

2. A _strong_ test indicates a need for a _change_ from the client's habitual water consumption pattern. A weak test indicates that the water supply currently consumed is adequate for the person's health needs. (Think of it as asking the question "Do you need to change the type of water you drink on a regular basis?)

3. If indicated, test for a type of water that would be beneficial.

Figure 8: Test for Water Quality

TESTING FOR ELECTROMAGNETIC POLLUTION

Overhead power lines, airwave communications, fluorescent lights, computers, hair dryers and other appliances constantly bombard us with electromagnetic field (EMF) pollution. The potentially harmful electromagnetic field set up by alternating currents interferes with a person's own electromagnetic energy field and nervous system.

Many people experience weakness, suffer from headaches, or just feel generally ill when they work in front of computers or under fluorescent lights all day. They may never feel as good as they would like, because of the effects of electromagnetic fields generated by their computers or illumination. Some of the effects of this constant bombardment of EMF pollution on the body include fatigue, headaches, carpal tunnel syndrome, tennis elbow, and arthritis – all due to the weakening of one's energy field.

When the energy field is weakened, the arterial blood becomes more acidic. The normal pH (acidity rating) of the blood should be 7.36 $\pm$ .05. After constant exposure to EMF, blood acidity rises and can create an environment that is amenable to pathogenic organisms such as viruses, parasites and bacteria. Cancer thrives in an acidic body.

Wearing a small multipolar magnet in your pocket can prevent some of the ill effects of this loss of personal electromagnetic energy and EMF bombardment. Place the magnet, cloth side in, against the body. It generally takes only one multipolar magnet card to provide inexpensive protection. Qlinks have also been shown in many studies to protect your body from the effects of EMF's.

Testing Procedure:
1. Test the muscle in the clear.
2. Expose the person being tested to an electromagnetic field, such as a cell phone (Figure 9), computer, hair dryer, or fluorescent lighting.
3. If the client tests weak, then retest. Have the person hold a magnet or put on a Qlink necklace or bracelet and repeat Step 2. If the muscle strengthens, then your client's body is communicating that wearing a magnet or Qlink during the day would be beneficial.

Figure 9: Cell Phone EMF test

Let's stop a moment and review what you have learned. Good for you for sticking with it. You have been given a lot of new information, and I am sure there is a lot here to digest. I do not want to overwhelm you, so take a few moments and have fun with these practice exercises. Remember: The more you practice, the easier it will become, and the more your confidence will grow. (True confession: It took me awhile to master this, too!)

PRACTICE SESSION 1:

1. Ask for the person's permission to be tested.
2. Find a test muscle and test it in the clear. (Do this before adding any outside influences.)
3. Do Testing Readiness Process. (Have your client put their fingers together in a bunch and test and then apply to the middle of the forehead and test.)
4. Check their polarity on the dip below glabella protrusion.
5. Check hydration on the tip of scapula.
6. Check water quality. (Tug ear up and out. If the muscle tests weak, no change is needed.)

7. Check electromagnetic field sensitivity. (Use a cell phone or other electronic devise.)

8. Practice these procedures on several other people to gain more experience.

PRACTICE SESSION NUMBER 2:

1. Find test muscle, and test in the clear.
2. Use Testing Readiness Process.
3. Test polarity point.
4. Practice finding landmarks on the body by trying to find each organ sweep point and testing each point. (See Chapter 5 to review "Body Landmarks" and "Organ Sweep.")

TESTING FOR PRIORITY

When it comes to health concerns, people are often divided into two groups: the first wants a quick fix for bothersome or painful symptoms; the second wants a long-term program that maintains or even increases general vitality and health. Consider all of this when you test a person. Realize that each person has a uniquely personal health concern. In addition, each person's body wisdom has several concerns it wants to focus on. I call this focus the body's "Priority."

The Priority indicates the health concern on which the client is most able and willing to work. It takes into account lifestyle choices relating to what the client is willing to do, both consciously and unconsciously, in an effort to stay well. For example, is the person's willing to add supplements to the diet, or stop eating certain foods? Will your client quit smoking, and is he or she committed to spending the time, effort and money in an attempt to achieve wellness? Do the ideas of exercise and diet fit into the client's idea of a healthy lifestyle?

Given all the areas that could be treated, Priority is what the client's body-wisdom indicates it wants to work on first. In most cases, the Priority indicates an area in which the possibility for improvement is greatest and/or most accessible. Using the Priority hand pose identifies and anchors the nervous system's attention on an imbalance that prevents the body from achieving its greatest goal. What is most intriguing is that all the priority points are found in the facial region.

The Priority hand pose (Figure 10) identifies what the person's body wisdom is ready to work on first. For example, you might be ready to work on a painful area first before addressing a serious heart problem, which is more life-threatening. Then, after the pain is addressed, your body wisdom will address the next priority.

The Priority hand pose must be used simultaneously with other monitor circuits. It does not stand alone, but acts as a fine screen for these points. Once the Priority is identified, you no longer need to hold the hand pose. At that point, begin to test therapies that would suggest a path to directly remedy the problem affecting the weak circuit. You may also use this pose with any weak monitor circuit found.

PRIORITY HAND POSE

Touch thumb tip to lateral aspect of middle phalanx of index finger. Continue to hold the hand pose while touching the nine priority circuits listed on the following page, one at a time. Remember: *There is only one priority at a time, and you are looking for the weak monitor point.*

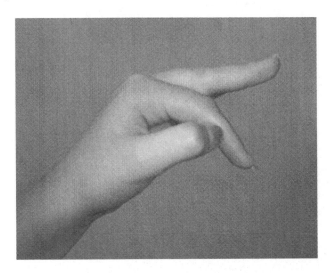

Figure 10: Priority Hand Pose

Here is an example of another way to use the Priority Hand Pose: Recently, I was visited by a client with a sore knee. I had several choices for how to proceed – I could randomly touch several places around the knee until the test muscle went weak, and/or I could touch the General Joint or the General Ligament point, or even each muscle that surrounds the knee. As it turned out, one or more of these areas tested weak. When a weak point was found, I held the Priority hand pose and retested the weak point. When the muscle remained weak, then I knew that was the best point to begin testing for various therapies to bring relief to the problem area.

PRIORITY FIRST LEVEL CIRCUITS

The Priority Circuits provide a fast and reliable way to direct body-wisdom's focus of attention.

The Priority Circuits have two levels: The Nine Primary Points on this page and the list of Secondary Detail Priority Points found on subsequent pages. Use the Priority hand pose while testing the points listed below until one point is found to be weak. If we were to test these points without the hand pose, several would likely be weak.

When one of the primary points tests weak, use the secondary lists on the following pages to further isolate the imbalance *while still holding the Priority Hand Pose.*

Touch each of the nine points listed below while holding the Priority hand pose.
1. Four fingers superior to level of frontal eminence, 2 fingers lateral to midline, bilateral simultaneously. (Hold your index and middle fingers side by side.)
2. One finger inferior to level of frontal eminence, 2 fingers lateral to midline, bilateral simultaneously.
3. Two fingers inferior to level of frontal eminence, 2 fingers lateral to midline, bilateral simultaneously.
4. Midline, 4 fingers inferior to level of frontal eminence.
5. Two fingers superior to glabella protrusion, 2 fingers lateral to midline bilateral simultaneously.
6. One finger superior to glabella protrusion, 2 fingers lateral to midline bilateral simultaneously.
7. One-fourth the distance inferior from glabella protrusion to tip of nose, one finger lateral to midline, bilateral simultaneously.
8. Midline, I finger inferior to midpoint of nose.
9. Bony corners of the chin, bilateral simultaneously.

For example, if Point Number I above tests weak, one of the monitor circuits listed under section one on the next page is your key to finding the priority imbalance. Test each point in that group and retest until one is found to be weak. Use that point to confirm for therapies. *There will be only one priority at a time. If you get more than one, check for switching and repeat procedure. Remember to continue to hold the priority hand pose while testing the monitor circuits until you find the __ONE__ priority.*

Photo Dr. J

Practice exercise: Locate the Nine Priority Points on the above picture, then place the corresponding numbers on the face. This is a good way to learn the location of these points.

SECONDARY PRIORITY POINTS

The Secondary Priority Points will give you more details about the information you received when testing the Nine Primary Points. Some of the points on the following pages are bilateral, and can be touched on either side of the face or body. If it is necessary to touch both sides simultaneously, the directions will indicate that.

Primary Point One

Brain function:	1-2 intercostal space at sternum, bilateral simultaneously.
Brain parts:	Midline, two fingers superior to glabella protrusion.
Central nervous system:	Midline, 1 inch superior to border of upper lip.
Muscle tissue:	Midline, 1 finger inferior to episternal notch.
Myofascial:	Midline, 1 finger superior to midpoint of nose.
Vagina:	Midline, one inch superior to top of pubic bone.
Mammary:	Nipple (have client touch each breast).
Sinus:	Superior or inferior aspect of orbit on pupil line, bilateral.
Ear and middle ear:	1 finger anterior to ear canal opening (in front of flap).
Ear and inner ear:	1 inch anterior to ear canal opening

Priority Point Two

Digestion:	3-4 intercostal space at sternum, bilateral simultaneously.
Heart and circulation:	Midline, 1 finger inferior to level of frontal eminence.
Cardiovascular:	Midline, 1 finger proximal to tip of nose on septum.
Uterus:	Midline, at level of ASIS.
Liver:	Midline, 2 fingers superior to navel and 1 inch to the right simultaneously.

Thymus: Midline, 2 fingers inferior to glabella protrusion.

Lymph: Midline, 2 fingers inferior to level of frontal eminence.

Tonsils: Midline, 2 fingers inferior to tip of chin.

Adenoids: Midline, tip of nose.

Eye: Eyeball (touch lid, with eyes closed).

Priority Point Three

Virus: Midline, 4 fingers superior to episternal notch.

Yeast: Midline, 5 fingers superior to episternal notch.

Fungus: Midline, I inch superior to episternal notch.

Endocrine: Midline, 2 fingers superior to level of frontal eminence.

Prostate: Midline, on pubic bone.

Spleen: I inch lateral to point I finger inferior to midpoint between navel and level of ASIS on left.

Enzymes: Midline, 2 fingers inferior to lower lip border.

Priority Point Four

Colon toxicity: Midline, I finger superior to navel.

Meta-colon toxicity: Midline, 4 fingers inferior to xyphoid process.

Gastrointestinal: Midline, 5 fingers superior to glabella protrusion.

Colon toxic deposits: Midline, 2 fingers superior to tip of xyphoid process.

Priority Point Five

Bacteria: Midline, 2 fingers superior to episternal notch.

Allergy: Midline, 4 fingers inferior to episternal notch.

Tissue sensitivity: Midline, 2 inches superior to glabella protrusion.

Meta-allergy:	Coronal suture, 4 fingers superior to glabella protrusion, bilateral (tip of the ear, 4 fingers superior).

Priority Point Six

Nerve tissue:	Midline, 2 fingers superior to level of frontal eminence.
Peripheral nerve:	Midline, 2 fingers anterior to anterior fontanel.
Meridians:	Midline, I finger superior to tip of chin.

Priority Point Seven

Hormones:	Bilateral, I finger lateral to midline, I finger inferior to midpoint of nose.
Adipose:	Base of third toe, bilateral (on top of foot).
Joints:	Touch each joint.

Priority Point Eight

All nutrients:	While tongue touches inside of cheek, touch skin on outside of cheek.
Lungs:	Midline, I finger inferior to lower lip border.
Bladder:	Midline, I inch superior to pubic bone.
Kidney:	Bilateral, I and I/2 inches lateral to navel.
Skin:	Midline, level of frontal eminence.
Bone:	7-8 intercostal space on nipple line.
Hair:	Gently tug hair.

Priority Point Nine

Emotions:	Midline, navel.
Mind:	Midline, 2 fingers superior to episternal notch.
Spirit:	Midline, 2 inches inferior to anterior fontanel.

Additional Secondary Points

Test the blood sugar points bilaterally

High:	Left side, 1/2 inch medial to pupil line, eyebrow and frontal eminence, 3/4 distance cephalad.
Low:	Same point, right side.

EVALUATING LEVELS OF IMBALANCE

Using the monitor points to gauge imbalances will yield good information about your client at a dense body or symptomatic level. However, you can also determine finer levels of imbalance by using hand poses to enhance the tests. With this method, you can pick up imbalances at very subtle levels even before they begin to manifest as symptoms. For example, you can identify the presence of a virus even before the person is aware of an infection at conscious level. (Remember: The body knows everything!)

To test imbalances at the **dense** body (symptomatic) level, no hand pose is needed. But you can get more precise details about the severity of an imbalance by using the hand poses to determine the scale of severity of an imbalance. The severity scale runs from minus-1 (closest to balance) to a level of minus-6 (greatest imbalance).

To test imbalances at the **subclinical** level – the stage in the development of a disease before symptoms are observed (this is closer to balance than -1)– have the client touch the thumb tip to the ring finger (of either hand) while you simultaneously touch a monitor point (Figure 11).

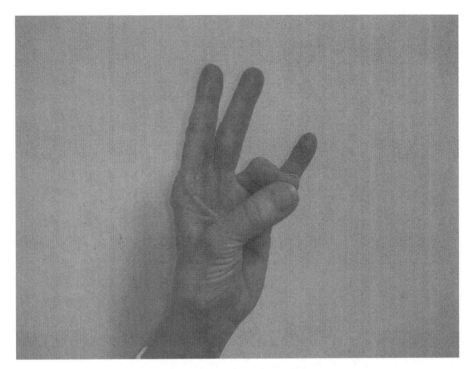

Figure 11: Subclinical Hand Pose

To test imbalances at the **<u>subtle</u>** level — the stage in the development of a disease where symptoms have not yet manifested within the body — have the client touch the thumb tip to the little finger (of either hand) while you simultaneously touch the monitor point (Figure 12).

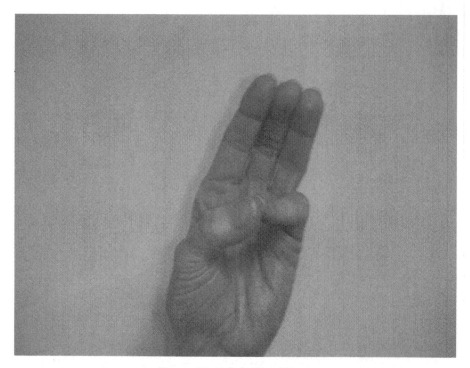

Figure 12: Subtle Hand Pose

To test imbalances at the **absolute** level, have the client touch the point four fingers superior to the navel while you simultaneously touch the monitor point. This is the most sensitive screen for determining if any imbalance whatsoever is present (Figure 13).

Figure 13: Absolute Hand Pose

Notes

- *These Hand poses should always be used simultaneously with another test; they don't work by themselves.*
- *Using a hand pose and using a monitor point are distinctly different processes, though the two are sometimes used in conjunction.*
- *Working up through the levels sequentially — working from absolute through to -6 on the severity scale — is not required and can be tedious.*

SCALE OF SEVERITY PROCEDURE

To monitor the severity of an imbalance or to track the progress of a therapy, we use the scale of severity. If a point tests weak without using an absolute, subtle or subclinical hand pose, then test with the following hand poses to determine the degree of weakness.

Minus one is closest to balance; minus six shows the greatest imbalance. Each hand pose will be weak until you reach the level of imbalance the next hand pose will test strong. The highest number that is still weak is your level of imbalance. For example, if a client's liver is a minus two, then numbers one and two will be weak, and three will be strong.

Procedure: (Figure 14)

While touching a weak monitor point, have the client touch the right thumb tip to the palmer surface of:

Minus 1: Proximal phalanx of right index finger.
Minus 2: Middle phalanx of right index finger.
Minus 3: Distal phalanx of right index finger.

Have the client touch the left thumb to the palmer surface of:

Minus 4: Proximal phalanx of left index finger.
Minus 5: Middle phalanx of left index finger.
Minus 6: Distal phalanx of left index finger.

Keep in mind: *The importance of these numbers depends on the area of the body being tested.* For example, a minus six big toe problem is much less serious than a minus five heart problem.

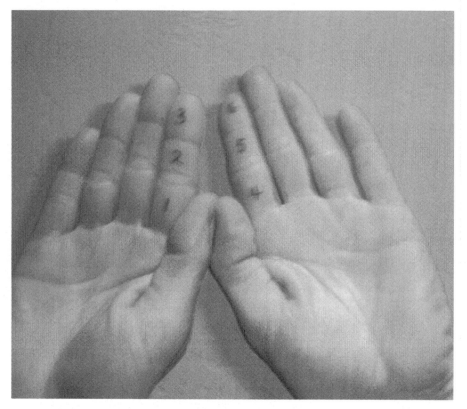

Figure 14: Scale of Severity

TESTING FOR TYPES OF THERAPY

At this point in the Wholistic Kinesiology session, you have identified the imbalance(s) in your client. Good for you! However, your work is only half done. Now it is time to begin testing the client to find out what he or she needs to do to correct the imbalance and find wellness.

The following tests will enable your client's body to tell you what type of therapy it believes will be most helpful. Put simply, a therapy is any action or substance that strengthens a weak monitor circuit.

When testing for types of therapy, please keep in mind:

- These therapies either take a positive step toward wellness, or avoid (or discontinue) a negative therapy that may not be working for your client. In cases where avoidance is appropriate, that action is often temporary. When balance is restored to the body, levels of tolerance are generally increased. For instance, a person may be sensitive to perfumes and avoiding them is good, but as the person gains strength and health they may be able to tolerate perfume a little more until it no longer is a problem.

- These tests are neither monitor nor standard-evaluation points. They are not determining an imbalance or whether a particular substance is good or bad. Much confusion arises with them. If you think of doing each pinch test as a substitute for the therapy it represents, this sometimes clears the confusion. A weak test indicates that the group is not needed or is not beneficial; a strong test means that it (or something in the group) would be useful.

Procedure:

1. Locate a weak monitor point.
2. After a weak monitor circuit is located, which indicates an imbalance in the body, touch the weak monitor point while performing the above tests.
3. When one of these five tests strengthens a weak point, some therapy in that category will be effective in treating that imbalance.
4. When more than one of these therapy groups is found to be helpful, use verbal testing to narrow down the number of therapy groups. Similarly, if several suggested therapies within the group are found to be helpful, use verbal testing to narrow down the number of possibilities within the group. (For more information about verbal testing, see Chapter 9.) Any number of these five circuits may test strong. This does not necessarily indicate using a separate therapy from each of the strong categories of therapy. Sometimes

there is an overlap, such as with acupuncture. For example, acupuncture can be considered bodywork, energy change, or emotional work.

I.**Interaction**: Factors to be avoided or identified and compensated for, including ingestants, inhalants, soaps, perfumes, lotions, textiles, sounds, colors, kinds of light and various electromagnetic factors. To test, gently tug tip of nose and release (Figure 15). Retest monitor point, if it strengthens the point, this group would be beneficial.

Figure 15: Pinch Test-Interaction

2. **Nutrition**: Food, drink and/or nutritional supplements that can to be added to or eliminated from the diet. To test, gently tug the lower lip and release. Retest monitor point. If it strengthens the previously weak point, something in this category would be helpful to rebalance the imbalance.

Figure 16: Pinch Test-Nutrition

3. **Bodywork**: Any corrective structural action directed toward the muscles or skeletal system. Therapies may include chiropractic adjustments, massage therapy, joint optimization, muscle balancing, changing shoes, ergonomics, surgery and acupuncture. To test, gently twist a pinch of skin anywhere on the body (Figure 17). Retest monitor point, if it now tests strong, something in this category of therapies would be beneficial to balance the imbalance.

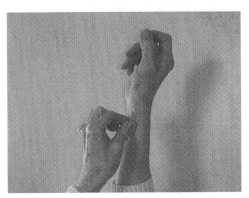

Figure 17: Pinch Test-Bodywork

5. **Energy Change**: Adding or modifying an outside factor that affects the body, such as exercise, sleep and work. To test, gently tug ear cartilage laterally and release (Figure 18). Retest monitor point, if it now tests strong, something in this category would be beneficial to help balance the imbalance you are working on.

Figure 18: Pinch Test-Energy Change

6. **Mind/Emotional**: Work with emotions, attitudes, fears and phobias. Some therapies include EFT, EMDR, NLP, Meridian optimization, counseling, etc. To test, gently tug the eyelid and release (Figure 19). Retest monitor point, if it is strong, something in this category would be beneficial to your clients imbalance.

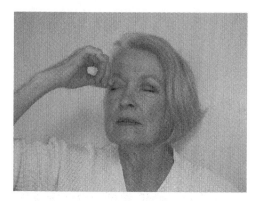

Figure 19: Pinch Test-Emotional Work

THERAPY SUGGESTIONS

It is important to remember that this is only a partial list of therapy recommendations for clients who test strong in any of the above therapy testing procedures. Each of the following healing modalities will fit into one or more of these categories and may be tested as useful or not.

<u>Bodywork</u>

Muscle Optimization	Joint Optimization
Chiropractic	Sports or KinesioTaping
Massage	Ultrasound
Acupuncture	Neuromuscular Therapy
Rolfing	Bowen Therapy
Traigger	Reiki
Trigger Point therapy	Surgery

Emotional Work

Counseling   EMDR
Emotional Freedom Technique   Acupuncture
Meridian Optimization   Reiki
Shock Release   Feelings Buried Alive
Be Set Free Fast (BSFF)   Neuro-linguistic Programming (NLP)

Energy Change

Exercise (more/less/different)   Sleep (more/less/different)
Work (Hours etc)

Nutrition

Change diet (add or delete something)   Vitamins
Herbs   Minerals
Amino Acids   Homeopathics

Interaction

Something in the client's home or work environment needs to be changed. It may be something as simple as changing shampoos, switching to a different brand of makeup or deodorant (or eliminating both!), or eliminating a perfume or cologne. Verbally test these suggestions, and if further exploration is needed, test the client's reaction to his or her carpeting, bed, etc.

WHOLISTIC KINESIOLOGY TESTING PROCESS:

A REVIEW

Testing Readiness Process tells us whether or not we will get correct answers during our testing session. If frequent neurological "switching" occurs, it will give us false answers when using kinesiology. This can indicate an underlying neurological imbalance that can be corrected with Cross Crawl exercises. The practitioner evaluates and instructs the client on the proper method of doing these brain-balancing exercises, which can improve the client's ability to function on a day-to-day basis.

The **Polarity** test evaluates the client's ability to give correct answers during the testing session. Someone who is in "overdrive" will react strong to all tests and will not give correct answers. This usually indicates an adrenal hyper-drive is happening due to constant stress. The practitioner may have the client chew some adrenal support supplement or some other substance, which will temporarily give the individual a balanced polarity point so that during the testing session, the practitioner can get correct answers to the questions that are asked of the client's body. Sometimes, long-term adrenal support may be necessary.

Hydration is evaluated because many people live in a state of extreme dehydration. Water is so very important to our functioning ability. Many health conditions can be remedied by just drinking enough water. Our correct answers from the body are dependent on the conductivity of the nerve signals. These signals cannot flow correctly when the body is in a state of dehydration.

Water quality is a whole other issue. The drinking water that comes out of the tap is generally not fit for human consumption. Having pure clean water is essential to good health. This is why the practitioner evaluates the client's current source of water and recommends changes if needed.

Electromagnetics are evaluated because of the huge impact electromagnetic energy has on our bodies. We are constantly bombarded with electromagnetic energy from cell phones, lighting systems, utility lines and computers, among other gadgets. Wearing a multi-polar magnet can help alleviate some of the stress this energy places on our bodies. Magnets are especially recommended for those who spend a lot of time in front of a computer.

Organ Sweep evaluates how each organ is functioning. This can be done after the priorities are balanced or before. Ask your practitioner if you have questions about particular areas of concern. Those areas where imbalances are found will be noted and reevaluated next visit.

Priorities are those areas that the client's body has chosen to work on first. Working on these areas will give the client the most efficient route to restoring balance in the body. The priorities may change from visit to visit, as the practitioner begins peeling away layers of imbalances. Measuring the **level of imbalance** gives the client a way to monitor his or her progress from visit to visit. "Absolute" is the most balanced, while a level of "minus-6" is the most imbalanced.

Type of therapy is chosen from five different categories: Nutrition, Emotional Work, Bodywork, Energy Change (exercise, sleep, etc.) and Interaction (something changed in the environment). The body will choose the type of therapy to help it restore balance in the most efficient manner. Kinesiologists are trained in all of these therapy areas; however, they will sometimes refer clients to other specialists if needed to help clients fully restore balance to their health.

PRACTICE SESSION 3

Whew! You have a lot of new information to digest. So, let's stop a moment and review what you have learned, and put that knowledge into practice. After all, the more you practice, the more your confidence will grow. Try this practice, and note your client's responses.

I. Explore readiness.
2. Check polarity.
3. Find a priority using the priority hand pose and points.
4. Determine the severity of the imbalance.
5. By using the pinch tests, find out which type of therapy will be most beneficial to balance this priority.

CHAPTER 8
TESTING FOR NUTRITIONAL NEEDS

Now that you have tested your client and found problematic areas of the body, and you have determined what type of therapy will work best to help your client achieve wellness, it is time to find out what type of remedy — and the correct dosage and duration and timing among other things — the body requires.

HEALTH REMEDY PROCEDURE

This procedure is extremely useful for evaluating substances for effectiveness. Only the most highly beneficial and efficient remedies will pass this test. As with all other procedures you have previously performed, this point must test strong in the clear. Make sure to test this point before introducing substances for evaluation.

Procedure:

1. Touch the indentation in the inferior aspect of the zygomatic (cheek) bone (Figure 20). Test this point first by using the indicator muscle to make sure it tests strong before adding anything to evaluate.

2. Place a sample of the remedy near the body (within one inch is preferable), or perform a brief sample of bodywork or other therapy and retest.

3. If the substance or therapeutic procedure tests strong, it is a useful remedy; if the substance or therapy tests weak, choose another remedy.

The Health Remedy procedure can also be used for energy balances, nutritional substances, bodywork, and other therapies.

Figure 20: Health Remedy Hand Pose

NEUTRALITY PROCEDURE

The Neutrality Procedure evaluates anything that may be ingested. This includes foods and other ingestants such as mouthwash, chewing gum or existing dental fillings. This procedure will not evaluate anything that is already in the digestive system beyond the mouth.

This is an evaluation point and must be strong in the clear to be useful.

Procedure:
1. Touch the skin over the points immediately inferior to the lower canine teeth, at the gum line (bilateral), simultaneously (Figure 21). Test to make sure it is strong before using it to evaluate anything.
2. Place an item to be evaluated near the body and retest while touching the points.

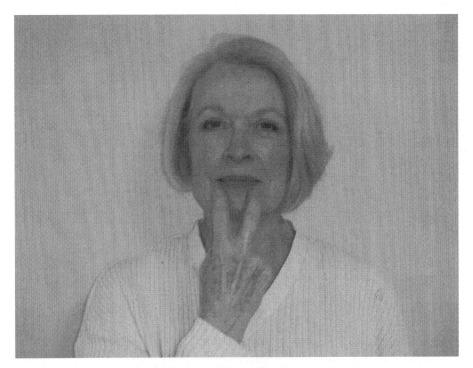

Figure 21: Neutrality Points

If a substance tests weak, it will not provide you with as much energy as you will expend eliminating it via excretion, sweating or other modes of ridding waste material from the body. It is generally better to abstain from eating this substance. If a substance tests strong, it gives at least as much energy as it takes away, even though it may or may not have some adverse effect at some level.

You may use this test to evaluate prescription medications, to help you determine if the medication has any detrimental side effects. If the medication fails this test, you may try to find a substance that helps with the side effects. Test it with substances until you find something that, when added, enables the medication to pass this test.

SAFETY PROCEDURE

This finer screen, which is more precise than the Neutrality Procedure, allows us to determine whether a substance causes a loss to any part of the body. This test can also be used to screen potential allergens.

This is an evaluation point and must be strong in the clear to be useful.

Procedure:

1. Touch the point 1/4 of the distance from the episternal notch to the tip of the xyphoid process on the midline (Figure 22). Test this point first, it must be strong before proceeding.
2. Place the item to be tested near your body and retest while touching the point.

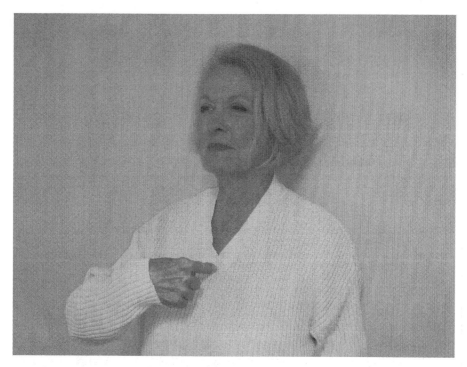

Figure 22: Safety Test

If the substance tests weak, then it is a detriment to the body. Avoid this product if at all possible. If the substance tests strong, it is at least neutral in its effect on the body. Combine this test with the Health Remedy procedure to fully evaluate a substance for effectiveness without harmful side effects.

PREFERENCE PROCEDURE

This procedure allows the body-wisdom to select the best substance or substances from among the items identified through testing using the Health Remedy and Safety Points. This is useful when you have a number of items that pass both tests for a particular imbalance, but you want to narrow down the number of supplements needed and select only the best.

This test only evaluates a preference. It will not tell you how effective something is but only will give you a comparison. Therefore, it is best used after the Health Remedy Procedure and Safety tests have selected the best remedies.

This is an evaluation point and must test strong in the clear.

Procedure:
1. Place all the substances we wish to test on or within one inch of the body, keeping them separated from each other slightly.
2. Have the client connect the tips of the thumb and index fingers and touch each of the items in turn, with the other three fingers together pointing down(Figure 23).
3. Eliminate those items that test weak.

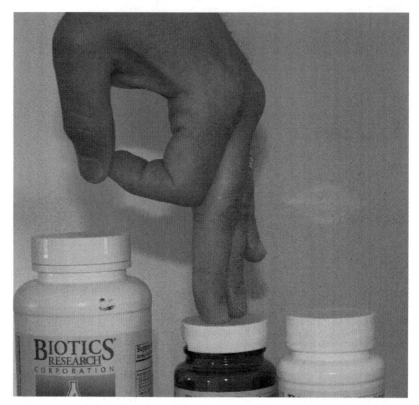

Figure 23: Preference Hand Pose

HEALTH COMBINATION PROCEDURE

This technique is used to select the supplements in a group that will work well together. It eliminates duplicate supplements as well. If you have two or more substances that are similar in action but the body does not prefer one over the other, this procedure may eliminate one or more of the choices. This procedure may also be used with foods or medications and may be used before or after Health Remedy.

This is an evaluation circuit and must be strong in the clear to be useful.

Procedure:

1. Place all of the substances to be tested close to the body but slightly separate from each other.

2. Touch all four fingers and thumb together and point at one of the items being tested (Figure 24).

3. Test each item separately; the test will be strong on those items that should remain in the group.

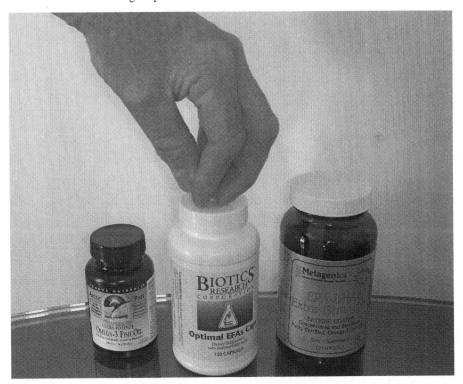

Figure 24: Health Combination Hand Pose

COMPLETE GROUP/COMPLETE PROGRAM PROCEDURES

This procedure will determine whether the substances that were chosen by the Health Remedy Procedure are sufficient, or whether more are needed to treat the imbalance. It will test strong only when the combination of items will fulfill the client's health needs. If it is weak, return to the Health Remedy procedure to find another remedy to satisfy this test.

This is an evaluation point and must be strong in the clear to be useful.

Procedure:

1. Touch both corners of your mouth with the index and middle fingertips (Figure 25). Test these points first before adding substances to be tested.
2. Place the substances to be evaluated close to the body and retest.
3. If the test is strong, the combination is complete and forms a complete ideal combination called a Complete Group.
4. If the test is weak, continue adding Health Remedy items or removing items until this test is strong.

Note: The Complete Group procedure could give any number of different but equally valid results depending on the sequence of items chosen to be tested. Our bodies are highly adaptable and able to use many different substances and combinations for its healing purposes.

Figure 25: Complete Group Point

COMPLETE PROGRAM PROCEDURE

This procedure will evaluate whether or not there are other modalities of healing needed in order to resolve an imbalance. This point will test strong when we have identified all appropriate therapies. In other words, your client may want some bodywork in addition to nutrients to balance the imbalance you are working on.

This is an evaluation point and must be strong in the clear to be useful.

Procedure:

1. With a complete group of substances near the body, touch the right side of the right eye (lateral corner). (Figure 26)

2. If the test is strong, the program is complete. If the test is weak, a different type of therapy is called for (if you have been testing nutrients-then check now for bodywork, interaction, etc.). Use the pinch tests (Figures 15-19) to determine which therapy is appropriate. When a therapy passes Health Remedy, perform a sample of the therapy and retest the Complete Program Procedure with the other remedies still present. If strong, the program is complete. If still weak, add another Health Remedy therapy until this test is strong.

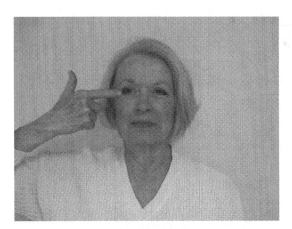

Figure 26: Complete Program Point

DOSING PROCEDURE

One of the key advantages of Wholistic Kinesiology over other modalities is that we can determine the exact amount of a substance that will be beneficial for each individual. We are all different in our needs and our individual biochemical makeup. Each of us requires different amounts of a remedy or type of therapy to help us regain balance in our health. Each individual's need may be less or more than the recommended dose of a substance or procedure. Rather than using a standard dose for everyone, this procedure allows us to determine specific dosing.

Once you have identified the remedies that pass the designated tests, the Dosing Procedures will determine how much of a substance should be ingested or how often a procedure should be done over the next 24 hours. Each remedy/type of therapy should be tested individually.

This test is an evaluation point and must test strong in the clear.

Procedure:
1. Have the client point into either ear canal with the index finger (Figure 27). Test to make sure this point is strong before proceeding.
2. Place one or more capsules, tablets, or liquid near the body. (The starting number may be an educated guess, or just start at one and work up.)
3. Retest. If the test is strong, continue adding the substance until you find a weakness. Reduce the number of pills or amount of liquid until the test is strong again. The test will be strong at the useful daily dose but will be weakened by too much of the substance.

Figure 27: Dosing Point

DURATION OF DOSE PROCEDURE

This test will indicate the number of days that the body can safely and effectively use the tested substance(s). In most cases, going over or under the amount needed by a few days is not significant. **PLEASE NOTE:** This test only takes into account **the current status** of the body. Many changes may happen between the time that we test someone and the time we retest someone. Therefore, no one can predict changes that may affect the accuracy of this test, but it is the best that we can do, since it is impractical to retest every day. Changes in such things as diet, stress levels, and trauma may affect the accuracy of the remedies and the doses. Instruct your clients to inform you if major changes occur, and then recheck their programs.

This is an evaluation circuit and must be strong in the clear to be useful.

Procedure:
1. Place the Health Group of substances in the dosed amounts near the body.
2. Have the client place the index fingertip onto the nail surface of his/her thumb (Figure 28). Retest to make sure this point is strong before proceeding.
3. While holding that pose, touch the following points in sequence to determine the duration of the dose:
   a. tip of chin – one week
   b. lower lip – two weeks
   c. either corner of mouth – three weeks
   d. upper lip – one month
   e. tip of nose – two months
   f. glabella protrusion – six months

While touching these points and holding the hand pose, retest the test muscle. The test will be strong up to the correct time period and weak when it is too long.

Figure 28: Duration Hand Pose

Once you have completed all these steps and feel confident that you have found a way to balance your clients imbalances, it is good to go back to the original weak point you were working on and make sure it tests strong all the way to the absolute level. (Use the point four fingers above the naval with the monitor point) make sure to have the remedies next to the body or have performed the therapy required before testing.

To proceed to the next priority, keep the remedies next to the body and return to the priority procedure again. (Hold the priority hand poae and go through the priority sequence again.) The body will give you the next most important thing to address. Proceed through the sequence of steps that follow until you resolve that imbalance as well.

As you gain experience and speed, you will be able to go through a number of rounds of the process until the body no longer gives you a priority. At this point you may go to the organ sweep and determine if there are other imbalances the body wants to address at this time.

CHAPTER 9
OTHER PROCEDURES

Here are some other muscle testing procedures you can add to your repertoire. These creative techniques will provide more information on imbalances detected in the body. With a little practice, the procedures can be easily mastered, and integrated into your kinesiology sessions.

INDEPENDENT FUNCTION

Each weak monitor point can indicate a chain of imbalances and, like the weak link of a chain, can be the one area that directs you to a bigger problem elsewhere in the body. But the weak monitor point can also be self-contained — in other words, it may not be dependent on other body areas or systems for its resolution. So, to determine that a point is imbalanced by itself, and can be treated effectively by itself, use the following procedure:

1. Find a weak monitor circuit, and hold the tips of your thumb, index and little fingers together on the point (Figure 29) while retesting the weak point.
2. If the point remains weak, the area represented by the point is independent of other imbalances and therapy directed to that point — and what that point represents — will successfully address the imbalance.
3. If the point becomes strong, the area is dependent upon successfully addressing some other imbalance.

Remember: To avoid confusion with this, when the test is strong, other factors may be causing the weakness we're trying to address, so that therapies will not be as successful. Therefore, when the test is weak, that point remains open to testing and thus to therapy.

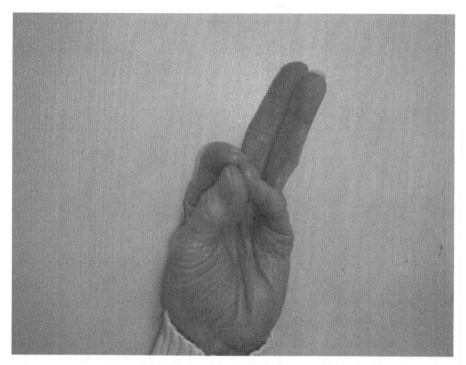

Figure 29: Independent Function Hand Pose

TWO POINTING

This process can establish whether any two monitor points that are weak are connected in a cause-effect relationship. For example, if another test indicates the presence of parasites, you can use this method to determine where the parasites are located.

Procedure:

1. Find a weak monitor circuit through normal methods. Then find another weak monitor point in a different location.
2. Simultaneously touch both points and retest.
3. If the test muscle is now strong, the two systems are related and have a common source of imbalance. The underlying cause could still be another undiscovered point, however. All you know is that theses two points are somehow related.

4. You can also use this procedure to scan for the location of infective organisms or toxicities by first finding the imbalance, and then doing a body scan until you find the area that makes the previously weak muscle go strong. (For example, touch the parasite point, if weak, have your client hold that point while you touch the liver point, colon point, etc. until it goes strong. This gives you an idea where the parasites may be located.)

FOCUS TEST PROCEDURE

This is an old prioritization process that was discarded some time ago by kinesionics practitioners. I began using it again because I found it gave me more information about a particular imbalance. For instance, if you come up with liver as priority and you want to know if the imbalance is due to an infection, a toxicity or deficiency, this system can help you with those questions.

You can also use the Focus Test Procedure as a way to find a priority, or you can use it as a final screen after you go through your priority points and all the monitor points in the body sweep. The procedure may help you detect another imbalance that didn't show up initially.

You can use this procedure in several different ways. Here are some suggestions:

Procedure:

Have the client place one or more fingers over the thumb (Figure 30) and test the indicator muscle.

Index finger – Imbalance is due to infection: bacterial, viral, fungal or parasitical.

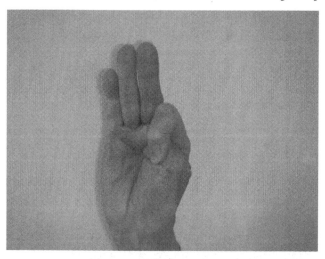

Figure 30: Focus-Infection

Index and middle fingers (Figure 31) – Imbalance has a metabolic cause. Consider further testing for problems in the endocrine system, adrenals, thyroid, sexual organs, pituitary, as well as digestive organs, liver or gallbladder.

Figure 31: Focus-Metabolic

Index, middle and ring fingers (Figure 32) – Imbalance stems from lack of elimination. Consider testing for problems in the intestines, kidneys, liver or ileocecal valve, or for candida.

Figure 32: Focus-Lack of Elimination

All four fingers (Figure 33) – Toxicity difficulties. Consider testing for candida, blood allergies, heavy metals, liver, colon, lymph or chemical exposures.

Figure 33: Focus-Toxicity

Middle and ring fingers (Figure 34) – Structural problems. Consider testing for musculoskeletal system, cardiovascular or organ damage.

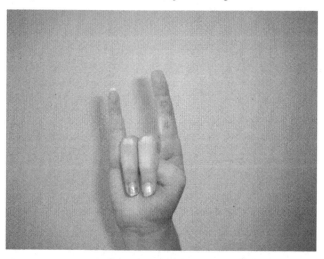

Figure 34: Focus-Structural

Ring and little finger (Figure 35) – Deficiency problems. The client may be lacking a vitamin and mineral or other nutrients in the diet.

Figure 35: Focus-Deficiency

If more than one priority is found during the Focus Test Procedure, have the client fully extend both feet as if pointing with toes (Figure 36). Retest each of the weak circuits. The remaining weak circuit is the priority.

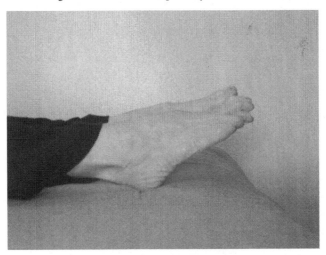

Figure 36: Focus-Priority

VERBAL TESTING

When testing the effectiveness of a substance to remedy an imbalance, Wholistic Kinesiology practitioners like to use physical samples of stimuli whenever possible. But when this is not possible, verbal testing becomes the next best thing. We know that people are often affected by visual or audio clues – reading or hearing words. However, even this method is not always perfect, for reactions depend upon the emotional meaning that someone assigns to certain words. For example, a man who almost choked to death on a raisin when he was a child will react differently to the word "raisin" than a woman whose kindly grandmother taught her to make delicious oatmeal raisin cookies. Different interpretations boil down to different experiences in life.

Keeping that in mind, I still would not shy away from verbal testing because, as previously stated, sometimes you have to improvise when you cannot physically get an item you want to test for. Plus, in the case of wondering whether you should refer your client to, say, a psychotherapist, you could use verbal testing and speak that specialist's name out loud and see if your client's body wisdom feels that person would be a good fit.

When testing verbally, remember to touch the points you are interested in testing while speaking the names of foods, supplements or suggested bodywork. This will increase accuracy and specificity.

Make sure that the question you are asking of the body is clearly a yes or no question. And make sure you are using a statement that both you and your client totally agree on its meaning.

If you are using affirmations, make them more powerful by stating them in present tense and in first person, and frame the affirmation so it is positive and life-affirming. For instance, do not say, "You will not smoke anymore." Instead, say, "You are a nonsmoker." In addition, speak as if what you wish to happen has already occurred. "I am eating a healthy diet" is much more positive than "I want to eat better."

Consult the book *Verbal Questioning Skills for Kinesiologists* by Jane Thurnell-Read (International Books, 2004) for more help in this area.

SURROGATE TESTING

Surrogate testing may be used when it is not possible to directly test your client, or when you are testing animals, invalids, babies or small children. But when using surrogate testing, make sure to test the person's body that you are trying to evaluate, and not the surrogate's. It is also important to make sure that all people involved are tested for readiness.

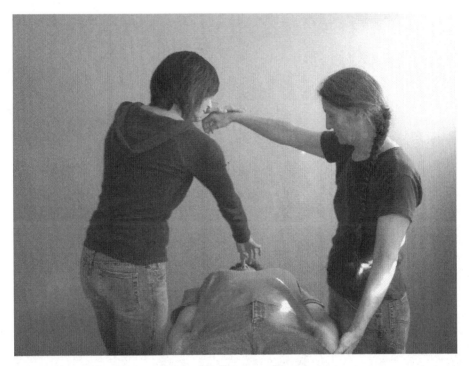

Figure 37: Surrogate Testing

SELF TESTING

You can also perform muscle testing on yourself in a variety of ways. Some people use the index finger to pull through the thumb and small finger of the opposite hand (Figure 38). Others use weights that are almost too heavy to hold, while still others use one finger on top of another (Figure 39). You can calibrate your yes/no responses by using something you know is good for you and something you know is bad for you. Once you are consistent with your responses you can hold something or put something next to you and test for beneficial or adverse responses to supplements, foods, etc.

The important thing to remember is to try to remain objective with your testing. Personally, I find this particularly difficult to do, because it is hard to not have any opinions about myself. I have found using another person's arm to test myself is more objective and reliable.

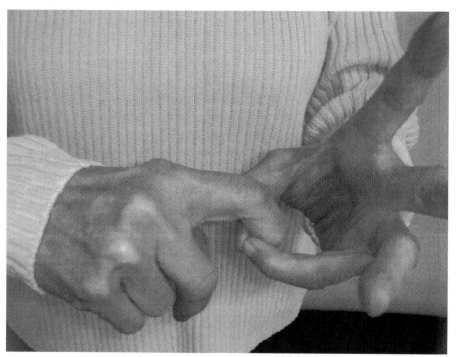

Figure 38: Self Testing Procedures

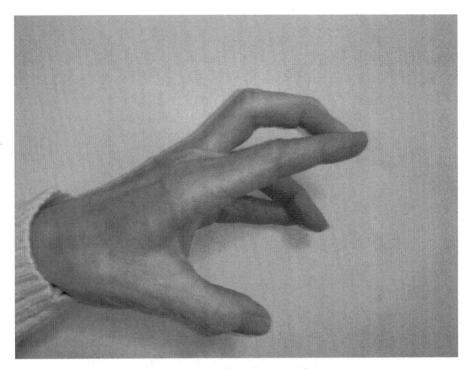

Figure 39: Self Testing Procedures

CHAPTER 10
SOME FINAL THOUGHTS

FIVE WAYS TO PROCEED

Using Wholistic Kinesiology, we can approach health problems in a variety of ways. The following examples present some starting points and the procedures for implementing them. Keep in mind: This is only a sample list; there are many ways to approach problems with this method.

I. Begin with a symptom or complaint. (i.e., a complaint about knee pain)

    a. Check Testing Readiness and Polarity.

    b. Find a weak monitor circuit (no hand pose) by either touching the area of complaint or finding a monitor point.

        Options:

        I. Two point connection with another monitor circuit.

        2. Scale of severity

        3. Priority

    c. Test a therapy or nutrient.

        Optional:

        I. Test the Five Types of Therapy

        2. Test the Health Remedy, safey, complete program, dose, duration.

    d. Do or apply the therapy.

    e. Retest the original weak monitor circuit.

2. Begin with any weak monitor circuit or point.

    a. Check Testing Readiness and Polarity.

    b. Select a weak monitor point from Organ Sweep or list.

    c. Determine type of therapy.

    d. Check Health Remedy, safety, dose, duration

    e. Recheck initial weak circuit.

3. Let the body speak!!
   a. Check Testing Readiness and Polarity.
   b. Choose Priority.
   c. Check Five Types of Therapy
   d. Do or apply therapy.
   e. Retest initial weak priority circuit.

4. Use a therapy that passes the Health Remedy test, as a general aid to good health.
   a. Check Testing Readiness and Polarity.
   b. Do or apply therapy.

5. Let the body choose a therapy.
   a. Check Testing Readiness and Polarity.
   b. Check Five Types of Therapy.
   c. Check Health Remedy, safety, dose, duration.
   d. Do or apply therapy.

IMPORTANT CONSIDERATIONS

For both legal and ethical reasons, Wholistic Kinesiologists should not use disease names or suggest (prescribe) any substance or therapy as a cure for any particular problem. Using medical terms to diagnose a disease is a punishable offense that can earn you jail time for practicing medicine without a license.

Wholistic Kinesiology gives a very specific and accurate description of someone's present condition, and it shows what will help him or her regain balance in his or her body systems. The point is that we do not ultimately know how the body works. We only know that a specific therapy, when tested against a particular monitor point, strengthens that point. We really do not ultimately know why. We should only observe what the body is trying to tell us and use that information to help clients regain their health without making judgment as to whether it is right or wrong, and without diagnosing a disease process.

People may on occasion forget to take their supplements or forget instructions that you have given them. It is important to remember that this is their journey to wellness, not yours. Your reaction is very important in their determining if they will want to return to your office or not. A judgmental attitude does not encourage people to continue working with their body-wisdom, which could eventually lead them to a healthier place.

In conclusion:

I hope you enjoy using these techniques to help others achieve optimal health. Do not underestimate the power of using the body to give feedback about what it needs. I have seen miracles occur on a daily basis just using these simple techniques described in this manual. Our body wisdom is awesome and we are only just beginning to scratch the surface of possibilities. If I have served to make the world a better place by empowering you to help others then my task is complete. It is at this level that we make the world a better, more balanced, healthier place to be. If we can spread the word and give each other healing there are no limits! Please pass the word!

If you enjoyed this manual and want to learn more, our 6 month course in Albuquerque is an excellent place to start. There are other amazing techniques in the Wholistic Kinesiology repertoire that complement what you have started here.

Yours in health and balance!

Dr. J Dunn
January 2009

APPENDIX A
WHOLISTIC KINESIOLOGY
EVALUATION FORM

The following two pages are the front and back of the forms we use in our clinic to record the results of our evaluation. We copy the front for our files and give the original form to the client for their own information. (The second page may look familiar – it was also reproduced as a helpful review at the end of Chapter 7.)

WHOLISTIC KINESIOLOGY EVALUATION FORM

Name_____Date_____

Practitioner_____

Exploring Readiness	_____OK _____switches frequently-Crosscrawl needed.
Polarity	_____OK _____needs support
Hydration	_____OK _____Drink more-(I/2 wt. in oz recommended)
Water Quality	_____OK _____Change Needed_____
Electromagnetics	_____OK _____Magnet needed

1st Priority_____
      Level: absolute subtle   subclinical   -I -2 -3 -4 -5 -6
      Type of Therapy/Remedy: N E EC B I _____

2nd Priority _____
      Level: absolute   subtle subclinical   -I -2 -3 -4 -5 -6
      Type of Therapy/Remedy: N E EC B I_____

3rd Priority _____
      Level: absolute   subtle subclinical   -I -2 -3 -4 -5 -6
      Type of Therapy/Remedy: N E EC B I _____

4th Priority _____

    Level: absolute   subtle   subclinical   -1 -2 -3 -4 -5 -6

    Type of Therapy/Remedy: N E EC B I _____

Organ Sweep: _____after priorities _____before priorities (*Note: These are kinesiology reflex points and are not to be considered diagnoses, they indicate relative functioning/balance of these systems*).

Prostate	Vagina	Bladder	Heavy Metals
Ovaries	Estrogen	Progesterone	Uterus
Cardiovascular	Ileocecal Valve	Ileum	Kidney
Pancreas	Colon	Gallbladder	Stomach
Liver	Spleen	Parasite	Adrenal M.
Adrenal C.	Candida	HCL	Implanted Virus
Lung	Allergy	Digestion (general)	Virus (acute)
Heart	Lymph	Thymus	Thyroid
Fungus	Bacteria	General Nutrition	Sinus
Pituitary	Blood sugar (high)	Blood sugar (low)	Assimilation

Other _____

Homework/Lifestyle changes recommended:_____

_____

_____

Comments: _____

BUT, WHAT DOES IT ALL MEAN?

Testing Readiness Process tells us whether or not we will get correct answers during our testing session. If frequent neurological "switching" occurs, it will give us false answers when using kinesiology. This can indicate an underlying neurological imbalance that can be corrected with Cross Crawl exercises. The practitioner evaluates and instructs the client on the proper method of doing these exercises, which can improve the client's ability to function on a day-to-day basis.

The **Polarity** test evaluates the client's ability to give correct answers during the testing session. Someone who is in "overdrive" will react strong to all tests and will not give correct answers. This usually indicates an adrenal hyper-drive is happening due to constant stress. The practitioner may have the client chew DSF or some other substance, which will temporarily give the individual a balanced polarity point so that during the testing session, the practitioner can get correct answers to the questions that are asked of the client's body. Sometimes, long-term adrenal support may be necessary.

Hydration is evaluated because many people live in a state of extreme dehydration. Water is so very important to our functioning ability. Many health conditions can be remedied by just drinking enough water.

Water quality is a whole other issue. The drinking water that comes out of the tap is generally not fit for human consumption. Having pure clean water is essential to good health. This is why the practitioner evaluates the client's current source of water and recommends changes if needed.

Electromagnetics are evaluated because of the huge impact electromagnetic energy has on our bodies. We are constantly bombarded with electromagnetic energy from cell phones, lighting systems, utility lines and computers, among other gadgets. Wearing a multi-polar magnet can help alleviate some of the stress this energy places on our bodies. Magnets are especially recommended for those who spend a lot of time in front of a computer.

Organ Sweep evaluates how each organ is functioning. This can be done after the priorities are balanced or before. Ask your practitioner if you have questions about particular areas of concern. Those areas where imbalances are found will be circled and reevaluated next visit.

Priorities are those areas that the client's body has chosen to work on first. Working on these areas will give the client the most efficient route to restoring balance in the body. The priorities may change from visit to visit, as the practitioner begins peeling away layers of imbalances. Measuring the **level of imbalance** gives the client a way to monitor his or her progress from visit to visit. "Absolute" is the most balanced, while a level of "minus-6" is the most imbalanced.

Type of therapy is chosen from five different categories: Nutrition, Emotional Work, Bodywork, Energy Change (exercise, sleep, etc.) and Interaction (something changed in the environment). The body will choose the type of therapy to help it restore balance in the most efficient manner. Kinesiologists are trained in all of these therapy areas; however, they will often refer clients to other specialists to help clients fully restore balance to their health.

APPENDIX B
UNDERSTANDING AND CONSENT
STATEMENT

The Understanding and Consent Statement is designed to provide legal protection to the practitioner by having the consumer sign a written statement of understanding and consent. It is also helpful for the client, because it offers the individual a record of his or her visit, which the client can consult and chart any progress.

The statement should indicate that the client understands that muscle testing accesses the innate body intelligence and that the information that comes up needs to be weighed by the consumer and as deemed necessary by the consumer or by a medical professional, and is not to be misconstrued as a medical diagnosis. The form should include a statement of consent to the session. The Understanding and Consent Statement could be a separate form or included as part of your Consumer Interview Form.

Whether an understanding and consent statement will hold up in a court of law has yet to be determined. Generally speaking, most practitioners and legal advisers feel it is better to have one than not. Please research the laws in your state and use these techniques within these legal guidelines.

EXAMPLE I
CONSUMER INTERVIEW AND CONSENT FORM

Name:_____Date:_____

Address:_____Birth Date:_____

City/State/ZIP:_____Height:_____Weight:_____

E-Mail:_____Phone (H):_____(W)_____

Occupation:_____FT:_____PT:_____Hr. per Wk:_____

Marital Status: Single:_____ Married:_____ Divorced: _____

Widowed:_____

Do you have children? Yes_____ No_____ If yes, please give ages:_____

Spouse's Name:_____Occupation:__

Physician's Name: _____(MD, DO, DC, OMD)

Phone:_____

Who referred you?

MEDICAL HISTORY

Date of last Physical Exam:_____Blood work:_____

Urinalysis:_____

Have you ever had surgery: Y_____N_____ If yes, please describe_____

Do you have a history of trauma, auto accidents, falls, etc.? Y___N___ If yes, please describe:_____

Do you have any spinal problems? Y_____N_____ If yes, please describe:_____

Please indicate below by marking as follows: I = present condition   2 = previous condition

___Headaches	___Disc Problems	___Diarrhea
___Dizziness	___Hip Pain	___Constipation
___Neck Pain	___Leg Pain	___Prostate Problem
___Lightheadedness upon standing	___Knee Pain	___Impotence
	___Ankle/Foot Pain	___Urinary Tract Problems
___Neck Tightness	___Arthritis	___High Cholesterol
___Shoulder Tightness	___Tendinitis/Bursitis	___High Blood Pressure
___Numbness & Tingling	___Asthma/Bronchitis	___Heart Condition
___Elbow Pain	___Fatigue	___Diabetes Type I/ Type II
___Upper Back Pain	___Frequent Colds	___Varicose Veins/Blood Clots
___Mid-Back Pain	___Allergies	___Other_____
___Low-Back Pain	___High Stress	_____
___Back Stiffness	___Ulcers	

Please list below any family members who have had the following:

Heart Disease_____ Stroke:_____

Kidney Disease_____ Diabetes:_____

Liver Disease:_____ Cancer:_____

High Blood Pressure:_____ Other:_____

Do you have skin rashes, irritations, or open sores? Y_____N_____

If yes, please describe:_____

Do you smoke? Y_____N_____ If yes, how often and for how long:_____

Do you exercise regularly or participate in any sports? Y____N____ If yes, how often
and what kind: _____

Have you had any problems keeping weight off/on in the past or present?
Y_____N_____

If yes, what do you feel is the most likely cause? Improper diet:____Lack of or

inconsistent exercise:____

Mental/emotional stress:____ Other:_____

Which, if any, of the following medications are you presently taking:

___Antacids	___High Blood Pressure Medication
___Antidepressants	___Hormones
___Aspirin/Tylenol/Ibuprofen	___Oral Contraceptives
___Anti-inflammatories	___Pain Killers
___Antibiotics/Antifungal	___Relaxants/Sleeping Pills
___Antidiabetic/Insulin	___Thyroid
___Chemotherapy	___Ulcer Medication
___Heart Medications	___Other_____

Do you drink alcohol? Y_____N_____ If yes, what types and how often:

Do you use stimulants (Coffee, tea, drugs, etc.)? Y_____N_____ If yes, what types
and how much:

Please list any vitamin/mineral supplementation you are presently taking:

Have you ever had a professional therapeutic massage? Y_____N_____ If yes, how

long ago?_____

Do you wear contact lenses? Y_____N_____

REASON FOR SESSION

What is the primary reason for your appointment today?

What results would you like to see from this initial session?

RESULTS TRACKING RATIO

Using a rating scale from I to IO (highest), please rate the degree of dis-ease, pain or discomfort.

Before Session: After Session

UNDERSTANDING AND CONSENT

I understand that the practitioner does not diagnose illness, disease or any other physical or mental disorder. As such, the practitioner does not prescribe medical treatment or pharmaceuticals, nor does the practitioner perform any spinal manipulations. It has been made very clear to me that this energy/body work is not a substitute for medical examination and/or diagnosis and it is recommended that I see a physician for any physical ailment that I might have.

Because it is important for this practitioner to be aware of existing physical conditions, I have stated all my known medical conditions and take it upon myself to keep the practitioner updated on my physical health.

Signature:_____ Date:_____

Witnessed:_____ Date:_____

EXAMPLE 2

EMPLOYMENT AGREEMENT

It shall be understood that _____is not a Physician and that counsel given is restricted to the correction of nutritional deficiencies or imbalances found through muscle testing and is in no way intended to diagnose or treat a disease or medical disorder. References to specific body functions or organs during the course of counseling are not intended to diagnose disease or medical disorders in that body function or organ, rather they indicate relative balance of that energy circuit.

In addition, it shall be understood that the methods used by the practitioner cannot necessarily be guaranteed to be successful, or without risks. I agree to assume all responsibility and agree to notify the practitioner of any adverse reactions to taking any of the supplements provided by the practitioner.

I can expect that any confidential disclosures I make to the practitioner will be preserved and respected.

I have read and understand, and agree to the above statement.

Signed_____

Date_____

APPENDIX C

USEFUL WEB SITES:
THE KINESIOLOGY NETWORK

www.kinesiology.net

Kinesiology Network is the Web site for Manual Muscle Testing, Kinesiologic Medicine, Applied Kinesiology and Specialized Kinesiology. At *kinesiology.net*, you will find useful information about manual muscle testing kinesiology, addresses of schools that teach kinesiology, kinesiology associations and journals, a muscle database, links to research-papers, and many links to other Web sites about Applied Kinesiology and different Specialized Kinesiology methods.

Address:

Kinesiology Network

Gästrikegatan II, SE-II3 62

Stockholm, Sweden

ICAK-U.S.A.

www.icakusa.com

The International College of Applied Kinesiology (ICAK) was founded in 1975 to provide healthcare professionals with information about the work of Dr. George Goodheart and the growing knowledge of Applied Kinesiology. Science and discipline continues to be carried out by the ICAK through its research and education programs.

Address:

6405 Metcalf Ave., Suite 503

Shawnee Mission, KS 66202, USA

Phone: 913-384-5336

Fax: 913-384-5112

Email: info@icakusa.com

ENKA-Energy Kinesiology Association

http://www.energyk.org/

EnKA is an individual and group membership organization dedicated to enriching, educating, and empowering energy kinesiologists worldwide.

APPENDIX D
KINESIOLOGY RESEARCH STUDIES

The following is a list of research studies that help to validate our clinical practice of kinesiology.

Applied Kinesiology Research:

Applied Kinesiology / Kinesiologic Medicine Research
Read more at **ICAK-USA** web site: www.icakusa.com/Research.html

I. Leisman, G., Shambaugh, P., Ferentz, A.
Somatosensory Evoked Potential Changes During Muscle Testing.
International Journal of Neuroscience. 1989; 45:143-151.

This study measures the way the brain and the central nervous system functions when muscles test strong versus when they test weak. Clear, consistent and predictable differences were identified in the brain between weak and strong muscle test outcomes. This supports the idea that manual muscle testing outcome changes reflect changes in the central nervous system.

2. Leisman, G., et al.
Electromyographic Effects of Fatigue and Task Repetition on the Validity of Estimates of Strong and Weak Muscles in Applied Kinesiology Muscle Testing Procedures.
Perceptual and Motor Skills. 1995; 80:963-977.

This paper describes the results of six independent studies. The research indicates the following points:

- Muscles identified as "weak" using applied kinesiology manual muscle testing methods are fundamentally different state than those identified as "strong";
- Muscles testing "weak" using Applied Kinesiology (AK) are fundamentally different than muscles that are fatigued. In other words, "weakness" is not attributable to fatigue;

135

- AK muscle testing procedures can be objectively evaluated via quantifying the neurologic electrical characteristics of muscles;
- The cause and effect of applied kinesiology treatment can be plotted over time objectively.

3. Perot, C., Meldener, R., Gouble, F.

Objective Measurement of Proprioceptive Technique Consequences on Muscular Maximal Voluntary Contraction During Manual Muscle Testing.

Agressologie. 1991; 32(10):471-474.

This French study measures the electrical activity in muscles and establishes that there is a significant difference in electrical activity in the muscle, which corresponds with the difference perceived of "strong" versus "weak" muscle testing outcomes by AK practitioners. It further establishes that these outcomes are not attributable to increased or decreased testing force from the doctor during the tests. In addition, the Perot study shows that manual treatment methods used by AK practitioners to reduce the level of tone of spindle cells in the muscle are, in fact, capable of creating a reduction in tone of the muscle, as had been observed clinically.

4. Lawson, A., Calderon, L.

Interexaminer Agreement for Applied Kinesiology Manual Muscle Testing.

Perceptual and Motor Skills. 1997; 84:539-546.

This study demonstrates significant inter-examiner reliability for individual tests of the pectoralis major and piriformis muscles, but not for the tensor fascia lata or hamstring, which are essentially simultaneous tests of groups of muscles. The primary importance of this study is that it demonstrates the reliability and reproducibility of muscle testing as a clinical tool, while also highlighting the need for clinicians to be aware of potential inaccuracies involved with the testing of some muscle groups.

5. Schmitt, W., Leisman, G.

Correlation of Applied Kinesiology Muscle Testing Findings with Serum Immunoglobulin Levels for Food Allergies.

International Journal of Neuroscience. 1998; 96:237-244.

This study shows a high degree of correlation between AK procedures used to identify food allergies and serum levels of immunoglobulins for those foods. AK methods in this study consist of stimulation of taste bud receptors with various foods, and observation of changes in manual muscle testing. The patient is judged to be allergic to foods that create a disruption of muscle function. Blood drawn subsequently shows that patients had antibodies to the foods, which were found to be allergenic through AK assessment.

6. Caruso, B., Leisman, G.
A Force/Displacement Analysis of Muscle Testing.
Perceptual and Motor Skills. 2000; 91:683-692.

Using a force transducer developed by Dr. Caruso, this study demonstrates the difference between muscles which the examiners perceived to be "weak" or inhibited, and those perceived to be "strong" or facilitated. This study also demonstrates that examiners with over five years of clinical experience using AK procedures were shown to have reliability and reproducibility when their outcomes are compared. Also, the perception of inhibition or facilitation is made in the initial pressure exerted by the examiner and this is corroborated by test pressure analysis using the instrumentation developed.

7. Motyka, T., Yanuck, S.
Expanding the Neurological Examination Using Functional Neurologic Assessment Part I: Methodological Considerations.
International Journal of Neuroscience. 1999; 97:61-76.

The authors discuss AK as a clinical measure of neurologic function. A review of the literature reveals methodological problems with previous studies of AK as a form of neurologic assessment. The authors discuss the problems with research designs that do not reflect the clinical practice of AK, which are common in the literature. They outline principles of AK and recommend that future research reflect more accurately the clinical practice of functional neurologic assessment and AK.

In addition to the studies described above, early studies are reviewed. While some of these early studies provide evidence in support of applied kinesiology, some failed to corroborate clinical observations common to applied kinesiology practice. Flaws in research methodology inherent in these early studies are reviewed. Requirements for proper research methodology and for adequate skill level of practitioners are reviewed.

Read the whole article: Motyka, T., Yanuck, S. (at www.icakusa.com)

8. Schmitt, W., Yanuck, S.

Expanding the Neurological Examination Using Functional Neurologic Assessment Part II: Neurologic Basis of Applied Kinesiology.

International Journal of Neuroscience. 1999; 97:77-108.

This paper proposes a neurologic model for many of the AK procedures. Manual assessment of muscular function is used to identify changes associated with facilitation and inhibition, in response to the introduction of sensory receptor-based stimuli. Muscle testing responses to sensory stimulation of known value are compared with usually predictable patterns based on known neuroanatomy and neurophysiology, guiding the clinician to an understanding of the functional status of the patient's nervous system. The proper understanding of the neurophysiologic basis of muscle testing procedures will assist in the design of further investigations into AK. Accordingly, the neurophysiologic basis and proposed mechanisms of these methods are reviewed.

Functional Neurologic Assessment and treatment methods common to the practice of applied kinesiology are presented. These methods are proposed to enhance neurological examination and treatment procedures toward more effective assessment and care of functional impairment. These assessment procedures are used in addition to other standard diagnostic measures to augment rather than replace the existing diagnostic armamentarium.

Read the whole article: Schmitt, W., Yanuck, S. (at www.icakusa.com)

9. Caruso, W., Leisman, G.

The Clinical Utility of Force/Displacement Analysis of Muscle Testing in Applied Kinesiology.

International Journal of Neuroscience. 2001; 106:147-157.

The goal of the study is to provide a physical record to support the subjective judgment that constitutes an AK muscle test. These records are perceptible to any interested observer and also allow the observer to distinguish clearly the two outcome states. That is, the images presented in the record by conditionally inhibited and conditionally facilitated muscles are unambiguously distinct. And the distinction must be rigorously quantifiable. Unlike the X-ray of the radiologist and the histological specimen of the clinical pathologist, however, the objective record will not be the source of the AK practitioner's judgment; that is, he will continue to rely on his trained perception of the event that produces the record. But the record will stand after the fact as a piece of objective evidence that others may examine in order to confirm the practitioner's judgment.

10. Monti, D., Sinnott, J., Marchese, M., Kunkel, E., Greeson, J.
Muscle Test Comparisons of Congruent and Incongruent Self-Referential Statements.
Perceptual and Motor Skills. 1999, 88:1019-1028.

This study investigates differences in values of manual muscle tests after exposure to congruent and incongruent semantic stimuli. Muscle resting with a computerized dynamometer was performed on the deltoid muscle group of 89 healthy college students after repetitions of congruent (true) and incongruent (false) self-referential statements. The order in which statements were repeated was controlled by a counterbalanced design. The combined data shows that approximately 17% more total force over a 59% longer period of time could be endured when subjects repeat semantically congruent statements ($p<.001$). Order effects were not significant. Over all, significant differences were found in muscle test responses between congruent and incongruent semantic stimuli.

The following articles are also worth noting:
Frese, E., Brown, M., Norton, B.J.
Clinical Reliability of Manual Muscle Testing.
Physical Therapy. 1987; 67:1072-1076.

Grossi, J.A.

Effects of an Applied Kinesiology Technique on Quadriceps Femoris Muscle Isometric Strength.

Physical Therapy. 1981; 61:1011-1016.

Haas M., Peterson, D., Hoyer, D., Ross, G.

The Reliability of Muscle Testing Response to a Provocative Vertebral Challenge.

Journal of Manipulative and Physiologic Therapeutics. 1993; 5(3):95-100.

Haas, M., Peterson, D., Hoyer, D., Ross, G.

Muscle Testing Response to Vertebral Challenge and Spinal Manipulation: A Randomized Controlled Trial of Construct Validity.

Journal of Manipulative and Physiologic Therapeutics. 1994; 17(3):141-148.

Hsieh, C.Y., Phillips, R.B.

Reliability of Manual Muscle Testing with a Computerized Dynamometer.

Journal of Manipulative and Physiological Therapeutics. 1990; 13:72-82.

Jacobs, G.E.

Applied Kinesiology: An Experimental Evaluation By Double Blind Methodology.

Journal of Manipulative and Physiologic Therapeutics. 1981; 4(3):141-145.

Leisman, G.

Limb Segment Information Transmission Capacity.

Journal of Manipulative and Physiological Therapeutics. 1989;12(1):3-9.

Leisman, G., Koch, P.A.

Cybernetic Model of Psychophysiologic Pathways: I. Control Functions.

Journal of Manipulative and Physiological Therapeutics. 1989; 12(2):98-108.

Leisman, G.

Cybernetic Model of Psychophysiologic Pathways: II. Consciousness of Effort and Kinesthesia.

Journal of Manipulative and Physiological Therapeutics. 1989; 12(3):174-191.

Leisman, G.
Cybernetic Model of Psychophysiologic Pathways: III. Impairment of Consciousness of Effort and Kinesthesia.
Journal of Manipulative and Physiological Therapeutics. 1989; 12(4):257-265.

Leisman, G., Vitori, R.
Limb Segment Information Transmission Capacity Infers Integrity of Spinothalamic Tracts and Cortical Visual-Motor Control.
International Journal of Neuroscience. 1990; 50:175-183.

Marino, M., Nicholas, J.A., Gleim, G., Rosenthal, P., Nicholas, S.J.
The Efficacy of Manual Assessment of Muscle Strength Using a New Device.
American Journal of Sports Medicine. 1982; 10:360-364.

Nicholas, J. A., Sapega, A., Kraus, H., Webb, J.N.
Factors Influencing Manual Muscle Tests in Physical Therapy.
Journal of Bone and Joint Surgery. 1978; 60-A:186-190.

Nicholas, J.A., Melvin, M., Saraniti, A.J.
Neurophysiologic Inhibition of Strength Following Tactile Stimulation of the Skin.
American Journal of Sports Medicine. 1980; 8:181-186.

Perot, D., Goubel, F., Meldener, R.
Quantification of the Inhibition of Muscular Strength Following the Application of a Chiropractic Maneuver.
Journale de Biophysique et de Biomecanique. 1986; 32(10):471-474.

Rybeck, D.H., Swenson, R.
The Effect of Oral Administration of Refined Sugar on Muscle Strength.
Journal of Manipulative Physiological Therapeutics. 1980; 3:151-161.

Scopp, A.

An Experimental Evaluation of Kinesiology in Allergy and Deficiency Disease Diagnosis.

Journal of Orthomolecular Psychiatry. 1979; 7(2):137-8.

Triano, J.J.

Muscle Strength Testing as a Diagnostic Screen for Supplemental Nutrition Therapy: A Blind Study.

Journal of Manipulative and Physiological Therapeutics. 1982; 5:179.

The Wholistic Kinesiology Center and Dr. J Dunn

Dr. J Dunn opened Wholistic Kinesiology Center, Inc. in 1995 in Albuquerque, New Mexico. Dr. Dunn is a Chiropractic Physician and Certified Kinesionics Practitioner and instructor. She earned her Chiropractic and Bachelor of Science Degrees at Palmer College of Chiropractic in Davenport, Iowa. Involved and practicing Kinesiology since 1988, she has developed her own technique: "Wholistic Kinesiology," which she now teaches at her clinic. This six-month course includes kinesiology, anatomy, nutrition, bodywork techniques, herbal studies, emotional work and business management. She also lectures around the world for various corporations.

Dr. J Dunn, B.S., D.C., CKP

Mission Statement

Our mission in life is to be of service to our fellow man and enrich the human spirit. We have chosen to help in a way that encourages the patient's own natural ability to heal. We provide quality health care individually tailored to the client. We believe in educating clients and the general public to help them take more responsibility for their own health and happiness. We have created a pleasant working environment for our staff and a vehicle for them to achieve success in all areas of their lives.

If you enjoyed this beginning course and wish to continue studying this material and become a Certified Wholistic Kinesiologist (CWK), please contact us:

Wholistic Kinesiology Institute, Inc.
9809 Candelaria NE Bldg 3
Albuquerque, NM 87112
1-505-554-7712
toll-free 1-888-236-2651

Visit us online at:
www.wholistickinesiology.com

Made in the USA
Columbia, SC
29 August 2024

40751540R00093